Just One More Thing, Doc

Further Farmyard Adventures
of a
Maine Veterinarian

Bradford B. Brown, DVM

TILBURY HOUSE PUBLISHERS
Gardiner, Maine

TILBURY HOUSE, PUBLISHERS
2 Mechanic Street
Gardiner, Maine 04345
800-582-1899 • www.tilburyhouse.com

First paperback edition: April 2007
10 9 8 7 6 5 4 3 2 1

Library of Congress Cataloging-in-Publication Data
Brown, Bradford B., 1929-
  Just one more thing, doc : further farmyard adventures of a Maine veterinarian / Bradford B. Brown. -- 1st pbk. ed.
      p. cm.
  ISBN 978-0-88448-289-5 (pbk. : alk. paper)
  1. Brown, Bradford B., 1929- 2. Veterinarians--Maine--Biography.
  3. Domestic animals--Maine--Anecdotes. 4. Veterinary medicine--Maine--Anecdotes. I. Title.
  SF613.B76A3 2007
  636.089092--dc22
  [B]
                                    2006039277

Cover photograph by Luli Emmons
Text designed on Crummett Mountain by Edith Allard, Somerville, Maine
Copyediting by Genie Dailey, Fine Points, Jefferson, Maine
Text printed and bound by Maple Vail, Kirkwood, New York
Covers printed by the John P. Pow Company, South Boston, Massachusetts

Contents

Introduction

This book is a continuation of my barnyard adventures as a veterinarian in Belfast, Maine, and for many miles around in all directions.

Every now and then a farmer would say, "Hey, Doc, can Junior ride around with you for a week or two or a month and become a veterinarian?"

And I would say, "It takes a little longer than that."

"What do you mean? How long would it take, Doc?"

I liked to answer, "Well, last week I couldn't spell veterinarian and now I are one."

But in seriousness, it takes six to eight years of college, which always surprised them. It also took patience, a strong desire to succeed, good marks and academic excellence, and good recommendations.

I didn't get into vet school via the excellent grades that you need today. Rather, I had some good grades and some average grades, plenty of determination and perseverance, plus a strong farm background, which all served to impress the vet school admissions committee. I also told them I would probably go into large-animal medicine. At that time such intentions were rare, since the pet-care industry was booming and a lot more profitable. The easier money is in Whiskers and Fido.

When I started college there was no formal pre-veterinary program at the University of Maine, as there is today at most state universities. So I chose to enroll in General Agriculture, since it would give me the chance to take the most elective courses and still include the core subjects I would need for medical school. I took history, psychology, technical writing, botany, agronomy, entomology, and a lot of courses in animal husbandry, poultry husbandry, etc. I always carried more courses than were required, and

I can't remember not running to classes or labs. It was the most enjoyable and mentally rewarding four years of my life.

I was used to hard work, and I continued working throughout college. The summer after I graduated from high school I went to work for the railroad as a section hand. We put in new ties under the rails and took out the old ones, which was harder than putting in the new ones. Then I would go home and bale hay until dark on the farm. The next summer I stayed on the farm and raised dry beans for college money. And so it went. During the school year I usually held two or three menial jobs like sweeping the gym floor, working in the laboratories, or working in the ag school dairy bottling and delivering milk, since the ag school had a lot of dairy cattle. I was usually desperate for money, but I was determined to get through college and then vet school.

After vet school at Cornell, I went into practice with my brothers Phil and Neal, also veterinarians, in Belfast, Maine. Neal soon left the practice to pursue a Ph.D. in pharmacology, Phil and I worked together for twelve years, and then I took over the practice.

My small-animal practice ended up supporting my large-animal work, which took place usually after I'd already put in a full day at the clinic. An office call was only four dollars, but I was busy enough so that it added up. Farm calls were a dollar a mile one way, with a minimum of four dollars a call. Once one farmer had paid the mileage cost, his neighbors would want me to stop by, too, because of the savings, and one call could easily turn into five, six, or more. I would charge a dollar or two extra for "while-you're-here" things like castrations and opening a cow's hard-milking teat. I also had to charge for medicines, of course, but I would cut the price of the medicine in half or discount it significantly for poor clients.

Many times I exchanged my work for goods and services,

mostly goods. People were always giving me eggs, potatoes, corn, cucumbers, and tomatoes, but I also ended up owning just about every ceramic configuration made.

I hear a lot of complaints these days about vet fees. Consider this: a veterinarian must buy or build a veterinary hospital and equip it the same as a human hospital, since it must handle the same situations. A vet has to provide a complete surgery with all the instruments, anesthetic machines, and other equipment that surgery entails; you must have an EKG machine, x-ray equipment, ultrasounds machines, and a good laboratory. Plus you need to have an efficient office for the paperwork. When you add that all up nowadays, it's often an investment in the millions.

It's probably safe to say that at one point I may have had the largest mixed-animal practice being handled solo anywhere along the coast of New England. When one of my friends asked me how long I'd practiced veterinary medicine, I said twenty-three years.

But another friend piped up, "Brad, that's not true. You worked so hard you probably put two years of work into every one, so I'd say you practiced forty-six years, at least."

What follows are some of those long, long days, when I never knew what "Just one more thing, Doc" might bring.

Bradford B. Brown
Vassalboro, Maine

1

Half-Done, Twice Over

I was called to examine a sick cow at the Boyce farm in the ridge-top community of Knox. As usual, it wasn't just one cow. After treating five additional cows for various minor ailments, I cleaned up and prepared myself for the next farm call. As I was backing out of the driveway, George Boyce knocked on the car window. I made the mistake of rolling it down.

"Hey, Doc, I forgot to tell ya. While you're here I wanted you to dehorn that damn bull. Killer's five years old now and he's getting real snorty. He's out in the old chicken house."

"Killer?" I asked.

"Ayuh, that's what the kids call 'im now," George replied. "They're real afraid of him. He nearly killed Raymond last week when he cleaned out his feed bunk."

Great, I thought. But as usual, the frugal farmer had a point. I was, in fact, already here. I turned off the car and radioed my office, asking my assistant to call the farmer who had been expecting me for at least an hour already and tell him I'd be delayed for another hour.

Grabbing my equipment out of the car, I chose three of George's many boys. Neal, the most reliable one, was about twenty-five years old, and I'd known him to be dependable in tight situations before. Our little band set off for the abandoned three-story chicken house across the field, the ground floor of which served as the bullpen.

We entered the chicken house and paused while one of the boys found the light switch. I stayed put for a few moments to allow my eyes to adjust to the dim light cast by a few low-watt bulbs. And there, in the far corner of the ground floor, stood our quarry.

Killer looked to weigh about 2,200 pounds. His horns, which were about a foot long, ended in sharp points. Cattle use their horns as weapons, slicing each other open in battle, and they occasionally injure each other accidentally when they're in feed bunks, popping out the eye of a neighboring animal with a twist of the head. You don't have to attend a bullfight to see the devastation a pair of horns can produce.

Cattle, regardless of sex, are usually dehorned when they're young, between two and five weeks old, and the horns don't grow back if the procedure is done right. They're removed either manually with a powerful set of loppers known as a calf dehorner, or with a burner. It sounds cruel, but after the initial burn, which kills the nerves to the horns, the animal no longer feels pain.

Our quarry in the corner didn't look like he needed much of a reason to tear me apart. Cattle have great memories about vets, and I'd blood-tested this guy several times. He'd learned the sound of my car, and when I was on the farm, he would start to roar and paw the dirt. He feared me and I feared him.

I asked Neal to secure the bull with a big rope around his neck and tie another, smaller one through his nose ring. The ring in the bull's nose was a sign that he was manageable; it provided a measure of safety for the farmer, allowing him to keep the animal at a distance by using a pole hooked to the ring. Neal accomplished his mission, and we fed the rope up to a ceiling beam and asked the other boys to tie it securely.

Meanwhile, the behemoth was coming to life. Killer was starting to paw the dirt floor and throw dirt over his back. He was well aware that something was different in his daily routine and started to test the fragile control we had over him. I told the boys up in the second story not to tie the smaller rope that went to his nose ring, because if he were to tear the ring out, which some would do occasionally in a panic, then there would be no way to control him.

We secured him as best we could, and I explained very carefully to Neal what we were going to do. To kill the pain of dehorning, I began by injecting procaine into the nerve at the base of the horns. We took a little break to wait for the painkiller to work, as you would at the dentist. After about ten minutes, I proceeded to put the dehorner on him. A dehorner looks like a bolt cutter. Mine had wooden handles when I bought it, but I had them replaced with steel handles because I kept breaking wooden handles dehorning various creatures.

I got in position and told Neal to get ready. It took all the strength we had to get the first horn off. Killer was thrashing about and pawing the ground angrily. The stanchion chain around his neck was hooked to a flimsy wallboard but the big rope around his neck was attached to the ceiling.

However, the fun was just beginning. Killer suddenly pulled the stanchion chain out of the wall, and only seconds later, the whole wall crashed down, bringing part of the ceiling with it. For the first time we realized just how strong he was. The younger boys, who had come down to watch, flew back up the stairs to the second story! Neal and I dropped everything and ran for the door. We made it outside, but the one-ton-plus giant was right on our trail. I turned into the yard and Neal took off behind the big cow barn. Killer chose to follow me.

I saw an open door to the shed adjoining the house and

reached it in a flash. Right behind me was Killer. In the shed I saw that the door to the house was open. I ran into the kitchen and shot straight to the front of the house where there was an open window. I jumped through it into the yard.

The bull followed me into the shed and stayed on my tail right through the house. Talk about a bull in a china shop! I never heard so much thrashing and crashing. The one-horned monster destroyed the whole first floor, butting into cupboards, the refrigerator, and the stove. He rampaged into the front sitting room and completely destroyed the farmer's tattered furnishings in a matter of minutes.

The window I had jumped through moments before still stood open. He hesitated there for a minute, pawing the floor. Then out came Killer, shattering the window glass and busting out the whole window frame. The sound motivated my feet to move faster, but I snuck a look over my shoulder. Killer was pawing the ground in front of the wrecked window, kicking up dirt around and over his back. Then he saw me. By now it was clear the animal was on a personal vendetta.

In Killer's mind, I was a matador without a cape.

Lungs heaving, I raced toward the open barn door on the second story of the cow barn, where George stored hay and machinery. It was accessible by an earthen ramp. I cleared the door and headed down the hundred-foot aisle. This was a no-exit strategy; only a doorless wall lay at the other end and in front of the wall stood two tractors. I determined to climb up on the tractors, where I could wedge myself between the rear wheel and the frame to put me just out of Killer's reach. I hoped.

But I could hear the bull's hooves thundering on the old plank floor behind me. I knew I wasn't going to make it up onto the tractors, so just before the tractors, I dodged behind an upright twelve-by-twelve post, the last one before I reached the wall. There I

Just One More Thing, Doc

stood, sucking air and shivering. Time seemed to stretch into slow motion. Not daring to show my face, I heard Killer snort before his hooves picked up speed. He charged the post.

At the last second, I hurled myself behind the tractors, and Killer smacked into the post with colossal force. The whole building shook like a minor earthquake, raining ancient hay chaff down from every crack. But the eighty-year-old structure had been built to last, and every plank held. Trembling behind the tractors, I heard Killer emit a groan, followed by a tremendous thud. I peered over a tractor seat to see that the mighty beast had knocked himself out cold.

As panicked as I was, my training kicked in. I knew he would not be down for long. I called to the boys, and Neal came running. He summoned his brothers, and I shouted to them to fetch my dehorner in the coop, and I took the second horn off. Now the bull was completely dehorned. We cleared out and watched from the door at the far end of the aisle. Minutes later Killer stirred, shook his head, and righted himself.

"How in hell are we going to get him back to the chicken house?" Neal asked.

I had already thought about that.

"You got a cow in heat?" I asked. The boy nodded. "Put a rope on her and bring her down to the chicken house," I said.

Neal ran off in the direction of the dairy barn, where the milking herd was munching hay, each cow in her individual stanchion. A cow "in heat" means she is in estrus, the period in which she is receptive to breeding. Soon Neal and his brothers were leading the chosen cow into the chicken house with a rope halter. They cleared a path through the wreckage and secured her to a post in the opposite corner of the chicken house from the bull's damaged pen. Distracted from his rage and pain, the bull trotted after her. Seconds later, he was otherwise engaged. We secured the entire building, closing off the damaged pen, and beat a retreat.

The boys and I managed to smile, and they trooped with me back to my car like the battle-hardened warriors they were.

When the dust had settled and we were all standing around the yard, in drove George's wife, Lucinda, home from a trip to town. A few of the boys helped lug in the groceries and when they entered the kitchen, Lucinda let out a scream that could be heard in the yard.

She hurried back out and asked George what happened. "Did an artillery shell explode in this house?"

"No. We had a little excitement while you were gone," George told her.

George and I and some of the boys followed her into the kitchen, where she broke down sobbing. Her first washing machine, which she'd bought with egg money saved over many years, was in two pieces, the wringer completely broken off. But she never held it against me—I'd escaped Killer with my life.

The community organized a public benefit supper for Lucinda's kitchen damages and, more important, the loss of her beloved Maytag. It was a huge success and provided enough money to buy a used, like-new Maytag wringer-washer and a new butter churn. There was also enough money to rebuild the partitions in the hall and kitchen and wallpaper the entire kitchen—a marked improvement over the whitewashed plaster that had served for a hundred years.

About ten days later I returned to the Boyce farm to treat a sick cow, and George's boys greeted me like combat veterans hailing an old comrade in arms.

"C'mon, Doc," Neal said, grinning. "Wanna show ya something." One of his younger brothers grabbed my hand and pulled.

I walked with them around the corner of the cow barn, where they pointed to a brand-new bullpen, designed to control the bull and handle him safely. George had gotten an FHA loan, and unlike the flimsy old chicken house, the new structure had concrete walls and a steel door enclosing a big open space, about twenty feet square. The boys said the bull was much easier to work with now.

"Nice work, boys," I said, rubbing the smallest one's head.

Afterwards I treated the ailing cow with an injection and minutes later I was washing up my gear. Just as I was stowing my gear in the trunk of my car George emerged from the barn, stroking his chin.

"Hey, Doc, hold up," he said. I paused by the driver's-side door of my car. "While you're here, Doc, there's just one more thing. I'd like to have my boar hog castrated."

"Why now?" I said.

"He's gettin' too big to service the young sows," George replied. "I think it's time we eat him. Unless we castrate him first, his meat will stink up the whole town of Knox. I'll risk it, Doc."

The reason George wanted the boar castrated before slaughtering is because the male hormone testosterone gives a rank taste to the meat of a mature boar. Worse, cooking the meat fills the house with a terrible, ammonia-like odor.

George led me to the boar's pen under the barn. It was in a crawl space only five feet high in the barn's cellar. I bent down to look him over. He was an astonishing creature, the largest boar hog I'd ever seen—about 1,200 pounds. He was about nine years old and had been servicing sows at the farm since he was old enough to do it, at around twelve months. A breeding hog's career can last until death if he comes from a good bloodline and stays in good health. Even after he's too old to have sex, his semen, if good enough, can be harvested and sold for artificial insemination. But on average, boar hogs are kept only for about six or seven years on a farm because they get unruly, become too big for breeding smaller sows, or because farmers want to shake up the bloodlines.

Gazing at the boar, who had impressive six-inch tusks protruding from either side of his snout, I realized that George had once more assigned me a task that involved the threat of being gored. Only this time the animal was at least twice as smart as Killer the bull. I quickly formed a plan.

I again asked Neal to be my right-hand man and told him to round up five of his brothers. When they had assembled before me, their eyes alive with the thrill of adventure and more than a touch of fear, I explained what I had in mind and what they had to do. Then we started putting the plan into action.

First, we dropped a noose around the hog's neck and wrapped the lead end of the rope around the beams of his pen, tying off the rope securely. He began to snort and growl, and I could see fear flash on the younger boys' faces. They jumped back to the other side of the pen, but then stayed put, eyes glued to their adversary. Neal and I secured the hog's hocks with nylon ropes as the giant pig kicked and squirmed, all the while screeching like a banshee. We held on, and the animal stopped thrashing after a few minutes. He lay there splayed out, growling and panting. I called two of Neal's brothers over and instructed them to hold fast to each rope. They seemed to regard this charge as a rite of passage, stepping solemnly into position and clutching the ropes as though they were tied to the stern of the sinking *Titanic*.

Breathing hard, I took a pound-can of ether and handed it to Neal. I jumped on the hog like a rodeo rider and wrapped his snout in a dry towel. Neal advanced with the can of ether and poured the fluid into the towel as I directed.

"Stand back, Neal!" I warned. "Stopper that can and hang onto it." I didn't want him to conk out on the ether fumes, which reeked in the surrounding air.

"P-U!" said one of the younger boys who hadn't been tapped for duty, holding his nose.

Just One More Thing, Doc

I struggled to hold the towel in place without snagging my hands on the tusks as the boar pitched and squealed.

"Careful, Doc," Neal said, "he's gettin' a little frothy."

He was indeed.

But in less than a minute, he slid to the floor in a heap. Immediately, he began issuing thunderous snores and snarking sounds, sending Neal's brothers into fits of giggles.

I dispatched one of the boys to my car to get another can of ether. Meanwhile, I told Neal to stand by and get ready to pour from the open can into the towel when I gave the word. Ether is fast-acting, fast-evaporating, and quick to wear off, making it relatively safe as a field anesthetic. You can keep a person or an animal down for a long time while dribbling small amounts of ether into a mask or a towel without risking an overdose. But the short-acting quality of ether has a drawback when working with large animals, especially if one is alone. If the animal starts gaining consciousness, it can start lashing out with hooves and horns before you can finish the job.

Acting swiftly, I disinfected the scrotum and made a rapid incision with my scalpel. In a few deft motions, I cut out the first testicle. But the ether was wearing off fast, and the hog stirred and groaned.

"Neal, give me the ether!" I shouted. But the boy, wary of the hog's tusks, jumped back, dropping the can. I leapt up and moved around to the animal's head with the hope of snagging the ether. I grabbed his head and reached for the can, but it was about six inches from my grasp. The hog tossed himself free. He regained consciousness quickly.

The would-be warriors instinctively dropped the ropes securing the boar's hind legs and he began paddling his feet. At that point I stepped clear, seeing I had lost control. The boy who was retrieving the second can of ether hadn't returned yet and had left the barn door open in his speedy exit. In my concentration I had failed to notice that.

By this time Neal and his brothers were huddled against the far wall of the barn. The hog charged by them on his way out the barn door, thundering toward his freedom. But the hog's adrenaline-charged retreat seemed to slap the boys to their senses and they took off after him, running down the long dooryard. The hog heard the beat of his pursuers' feet behind him and he picked up speed—his 1,200-pound bulk moved like a big bomb on four legs.

I have to relate a bit of background here. George's next-door neighbor, Kelly, was a crop farmer who, over the years, had seen quite a few of George's pigs, cows, and assorted other critters wander into his fields, demolish his corn, and root up his wife's flowers. Kelly had threatened to shoot the next animal that ventured onto his property.

Now I watched as the half-castrated boar hog barreled ahead, the boys in pursuit, straight into Kelly's yard. The boys pulled up short, tumbling over each other in a pile to avoid spilling into the off-limits territory. Farmer Kelly happened to be taking a coffee break on his front porch, where he kept a rifle at the ready for such occasions. No sooner had the enormous pig galloped across the property line than a rifle shot rang out. The boar hog dropped like a sack of cement in front of Kelly's porch.

Well, I thought, that castration's done.

"I warned you, goddammit!" Kelly shouted from his porch.

The boys turned their heads to their father, who had emerged from the cow barn during the commotion. George shrugged and said nothing, knowing Kelly was right. The boys knew enough to keep quiet. George nodded at them, and they ran to the tractor shed. In a few minutes, Neal emerged on the machine, entered Kelly's yard, secured the hog's corpse, and dragged it the few yards over the boundary. My work done, I washed up and got out of there

Just One More Thing, Doc

before George thought up any further adventures.

George and the boys butchered the pig, wrapped up the meat, and put it in the freezer. They hoped that, with at least one testicle removed, the boar would produce less of a stench in the frying pan. It was a worthy experiment, but it didn't work out. A family that size would have normally consumed the meat in just a few months, but because of the horrific odor whenever they had to cook it, three years passed before they took the final piece of pork out of their freezer. When I drove by I could sometimes smell the ammonia-tinged odor hanging over the yard.

About a month after the pig episode, I was at George's farm again. He'd just gotten my bill for the castration. Like many farmers, George examined his vet bill with a magnifying glass in one hand and a fine-toothed comb in the other, picking away at my services.

"Geez, Doc," he said. "You charged me five dollars to dehorn that bull. That's a little more than I thought it would be. Usually you charge that for two or three cow dehornings."

"Yeah," I agreed, "but this one was a little bit extra."

George paused, ruminating on that.

"You notice," I said, "that there isn't any charge for castrating that pig. I did half-castrate him. I could have charged you five dollars for that. So it evens out, doesn't it?"

"Yeah," George allowed. "Guess you're right, Doc. Fact is, I can't pay your bill this month anyway, because the ol' lady just ordered new sneakers for the boys. They were on sale at Sears and Roebuck, a dollar a pair, but I'll get to you next month."

Driving home, I got to thinking what a fool I was. I could have stayed at the animal hospital, castrated two cats, and made more than I made on that call to George's farm—probably the reason more vets were turning to small-animal practice.

I later found out that George had originally called two other vets to perform those two surgeries. They both had refused and referred George to Dr. Brown in Belfast. Those vets were saner than I.

I saw George in Waterville about ten years after I left practice. He spotted me and crossed the street to shake my hand.

"Dr. Brown," he said, "you were not only the least expensive vet but the best veterinary that ever stepped on my property. Wish you were still in practice. My vet bills today are astronomical. Your vet bills now seem like pennies compared to the dollars they charge now."

"I appreciate your words, George," I said. We stepped off in different directions.

2

Another Close Call

A man who owned a small herd of Hereford beef cattle called me. He complained that a three-year-old cow was acting crazy. "She's really nuts. Right now she's in the cellar of the barn. When the weather's bad, they can come in themselves; when it's good, they head out. But she's off in a corner by herself. I wish you could take a look at her."

"I may be able to get out your way this evening," I informed him.

He said, "Well, Margaret and I won't be around tonight. They're having their annual Christmas party at the Waldo County Hospital where she works; she's a nurse, you know."

"That's okay, John. Go ahead."

He went on, "While you're out here, Doc, will you vaccinate Butch? He needs his rabies shot. I'd appreciate it. I'll leave him in the kitchen. He's no trouble for you. You must remember when you saw him to remove that tumor on his elbow. He's a very kind and gentle dog. He won't give you a mite of trouble. Just leave the vaccination certificate and your bill on the kitchen table. Thanks and Merry Christmas."

I said, "Ditto."

I arrived at his little farm around nine P.M. I took my flashlight and headed for the barn cellar. Off in a dark corner, lying down, was a three-year-old Hereford beef cow. She was right where John said she would be. I casually went over to her and inserted an electronic thermometer in her rectum. It showed a fever of 105 degrees. I shone a light in her eyes and she went ballistic. She jumped up and started diving and cavorting all over the cellar, aimlessly and with abandon. She banged into things and acted as if she were blind.

I went to my car and got my thirty-foot lariat, hoping to restrain her by tying her to one of the cellar posts that held the barn up. The beam posts were about two feet in diameter. I managed to get my lariat around her two horns. Her horns were at least twenty inches long and tapered to needle sharpness. But after I got the rope on her, she really went crazy. She started diving around, falling down, and getting up. Then she started to circle. I had already tied the end of the lariat to one of the posts. She began to move clockwise around that post. In the process she was wrapping me up very tightly. At about the last turn around, she had the rope up on my chest and I couldn't breathe. I started to lose consciousness temporarily.

I don't know how Butch, the family dog, got out of the kitchen, but he must have heard the commotion and came down into the barn cellar. This really infuriated the cow. She became more delirious and dangerous. But now she began to go counterclockwise around the post in an attempt to get at Butch. This saved me from certain death, since I couldn't have taken the pressure of another turn.

Based on the cow's behavior, my tentative diagnosis was rabies. There's no cure for the disease in animals, so I secured the cow to the postand left the barn.

I went to the car and got a dose of rabies vaccine for Butch and we retreated to the kitchen. Butch was very patient as I injected him with the vaccine. I made out the certificate and also wrote out a note to John to call me the next morning at eight o'clock sharp even though the next day was Christmas. And I left.

At eight o'clock Christmas morning John called right on the dot. I told him that I thought his cow might have rabies. He was very perplexed; he wanted to know how it could happen.

I said, "I suspect that a rabid fox bit her when she was lying down outdoors. There was a case in New York where one fox was said to be the cause of fifteen cows dying of rabies from fifteen bite wounds. They'd been turned out into what they call a night pasture, because it was easier to get them in for the morning milking that way. All it took was one rabid fox."

I told John we would have to cut off the cow's head and send it to the state labs in Augusta for testing. I asked him if he had handled her, whether he had been around her mouth and saliva, and if he had any cuts or open sores on his hands. He said no, but it scared him so much that he took the injections for rabies protection himself. He was very upset over the situation.

The cow died Christmas night and the next day I went up and decapitated her. John and his wife Margaret took the head up to Augusta and we got a positive diagnosis of rabies. It was the first case of bovine rabies in Maine in many decades.

In those days the lab did the Negri body test. Serial sections of the brain are taken from the hippocampus and little black inclusion bodies in the hippocampal cells give proof positive of rabies. The closer to death the animal is, the more these Negri bodies show up. So in those days you had to wait until the animal died before you could do the test. If the animal was killed early, the Negri bodies might be absentt or too few in number for a firm diagnosis. Then you still couldn't be sure what you were dealing with.

A U.S. Department of Agriculture research scientist named Adelchi Negri discovered Negri bodies. He spent most of his career doing research on rabies for the department. Ironically, Dr. Negri died of rabies himself in 1912. It was the result of an accidental exposure from spatter that came from a rabies suspect that he was going to examine under his microscope. The spatter went into his eye, and he contracted rabies some time later and died. The Negri body test became obsolete when fluorescent antibody tests and immunoassay tests were perfected.

During the next year I ran into rabies cases involving another cow, a deer, and a four-month-old German shepherd that I have written about previously. All the cases resulted in death and were confirmed by the laboratory in Augusta.

After those experiences I got myself vaccinated against rabies, hoping to avoid a fate similar to Dr. Negri's. I also had a couple of people who worked in my kennel vaccinated at the same time. All the people who owned these rabid animals took preventative rabies vaccinations, if only for peace of mind. No one did come down with the malady and they went on to live healthy, normal lives.

If you see an animal not in its normal environment and acting peculiarly, you should stand perfectly still and wait for it to leave. You don't want to attract the attention of a "mad" creature. Animals in the final stages of rabies have a keen sense of heat, and if you stand still, you have less of a chance of being bitten. A suspicious animal should be reported to a public health officer as soon as possible.

3

Standing Like a Sawhorse

One day Walter called me from his farm in Union. "I have a very sick horse. When could you come out and see him?"

I told him, "It won't be until early evening."

He said, "He's acting very sick and he's stiff all over. His eyes are bloodshot and he tries to eat but can't. He's one corking good horse, Doc. He's the best draft horse that I've ever had. But he's awfully sick right now."

"You'll be my first call," I told him.

Walter said, "Just a minute, Doc. My wife Mildred wants to talk to you about our cat. She's got some kind of skin humor. The cat, not Mildred."

A "humor" is old Maine farm slang for any skin problem.

The wife got on the phone and talked about the cat for fifteen minutes. The cat had bald spots with egg-white-like stuff in the middle. His hair was all stubbly, and he had blotches on the sides of his face. She went on and on.

I told Mildred that I could take care of the problem with my double-barreled shotgun but she said, "You won't be eating here again if you do that."

So I said to Mildred, "Hold him closer to the phone; I can't quite see him."

She hesitated, then I heard her holler, "Walter, bring the cat over here and put him next to the phone." I would tell many phone callers the same over the years, and quite a few of them would fall for it.

I quickly tried to fix the situation. "Mildred, I'll have a look at him when I come in to look at the horse."

What she described could have been many things. So before I left the office I took some iodine pills and some thyroid pills and put them in my jacket pocket. If my over-the-phone suspicions proved true these items would be useful.

I arrived at Walt's at six P.M. He came out into the yard and greeted me. We went into the barn and there was Dick. The draft horse that Walter thought so much of was, indeed, stiff.

"Do you think we can back him out onto the barn floor?" I asked Walter.

"We'll give it a try," he replied.

Dick was very wobbly and uncoordinated on his feet. His hooves were stiff as well as every joint. We gingerly got him onto the barn floor and put him on a crosstie. I checked him over.

He had an elevated temperature, an elevated pulse, and his breathing was labored. One thing stood out—he seemed to have to concentrate in order to remain standing. His legs were as stiff as iron pipes and he was straining. As I checked him over I found that his jaw muscles were rigid, hard as rocks. They were also tender. The quadriceps of his hind legs were also sore and hard. The "quads" are similar in man and beast and have evolved to give the horse and man tremendous power. This is especially true in pulling or draft horses.

I stood back, looking him over, and about ten seconds later the lightbulb lit up. Sawhorse attitude equals lockjaw (tetanus). He looked just like a sawhorse with his stiff legs. His tail was straight out and rigid as a broomstick. It's a pathognomonic posture. (In medicine, this is a symptom that is always seen in a certain disease or medical condition.)

I went on to tell Walter that I was going to give Dick some massive doses of tetanus antitoxins along with cortisone and a painkiller. Then we managed to get the big, suffering brute back into his stall; it was a struggle for him.

Walter and I returned to the yard and he said, "Don't forget, while you're here, Doc, Mildred wants you to take a look at her cat."

I went inside and examined the cat and my telephone diagnosis was pretty well substantiated when I felt his throat. There was a lump on his thyroid, which is called a goiter in man and beast. It is usually the result of an iodine deficiency, but thyroid conditions are a very complicated study.

I left some iodized thyroid pills in her kitchen and showed Mildred how to give them. As we walked to the car I told Walt to call me at noon the next day and give me a report on Dick.

The next day Walter called. He was very encouraged; Dick had drunk twenty quarts of water.

I said, "Walt, you know how to make a bran mash, don't you?"

"I sure do, Doc. I used to make 'em 'bout once a week all the time for the draft horses on a Saturday night."

"Well, make one up, as watery as you can. And to the bran mash add three quarts of molasses also." He allowed he would. "I'll see you at around eight tonight and we'll repeat the treatment that we used yesterday."

"Okay, Doc," Walt answered.

I told Walt to call me every day at noon for the first five days after seeing him that night. On the fifth day I went back and Dick had lost almost all of that sawhorse posture and was acting more like himself. The muscles were softening in his jaw and his big quadriceps were getting softer, too.

While I was there Walt went up in the haymow. He threw down a bit of first-cut timothy hay, which is a particular favorite for horses.

"Watch this, Doc," he said. He went over to where Dick was standing and offered him some of that beautiful hay. The horse was able to get it into his mouth and chew it very carefully, very slowly, and then swallow it normally.

"Walt," I said, "I think you saved your horse."

A month later I told Walt he could start giving Dick very light work.

Mildred took a picture of the cat's skin six months later and sent it along with a note that read, "All healed up!" There was also a picture of Dick along with his stablemate doing the first mowing in the field, and that tells the whole story.

I must say that not all tetanus cases turn out that way. Most of them are fatal in man and beast. When I grew up on the farm we had a workhorse named Chummie who contracted tetanus. The vet came every day for four or five days to give him the necessary medications and feed him with a stomach tube. But Chummie went on to a horrible death. In Chummie's case he contracted tetanus from an old rusty nail. My grandfather had discovered it and removed it from his hoof about a month before.

Whenever I dealt with a puncture wound of any kind in all animals, I always gave a tetanus shot as part of the treatment, just as they do in human medicine. *Clostridium tetani* is an anaerobic bacterium that thrives in an oxygen-free environment (like puncture wounds) and is related to the culprits that give us gangrene and other nasty disorders. A shot is a small price for avoiding it.

4

Both Ends of the Island

One July morning I got a phone call from a man on Vinalhaven, an island off the coast of Rockland. Generations of Maine natives have inhabited the island year-round, and in the summer they are joined by vacation home-owners who have been coming for almost as many generations. It was my good fortune to have clients from both camps over the years.

My caller introduced himself as Brent Abernathy. "I've got a lame horse over here, Dr. Brown," he said. "When can you get over?"

My last call to the island flashed through my mind. Foul weather had nixed flying (my usual mode of travel to islands to save time), and I'd wound up taking the time-consuming ferry, which had chewed up eight hours on a busy day. On top of that, the call had turned out to be an expensive charity case. Charity cases were common in my practice, but at least on the mainland it was rare to lose an eight-hour block of time on top of drugs and services.

With these experiences in mind, I informed Mr. Abernathy that I would come over when weather permitted me to fly. "I should also let you know that when I come to the island, I'll charge for the call on a cash basis," I said as tactfully as possible, adding that he shouldn't be insulted by this request, as I'd asked the same from millionaires. He assured me that I needn't worry about being paid. I said I'd fly over the next afternoon if the weather was suitable, and he offered me the use of the private airstrip on his property.

The next day's weather was perfect, and the sun glittered on the sea below as I touched down on the small island shortly after noon. A middle-aged gentleman dressed in khakis and a crisp, blue cotton sports shirt strode over to the airplane and extended a tanned and manicured hand.

"Dr. Brown, nice of you to come," he said, shaking my hand firmly. "I'm Brent Abernathy."

I returned the greeting. Looking around I could see that my client wasn't in danger of hitting the welfare rolls any time soon. From his haircut and clothing to his gracious, confident manner, he bore the unmistakable signs of wealth. He was, in fact, one of the world's wealthiest men at that time. As we walked over to his car, a black Mercedes, he said, "After you take care of my horse I'd like to have you go to work for me."

"Uhh, does your firm hire veterinarians?" I asked. I had no idea what business he might be in, but whatever it was, he clearly owned it.

He grinned. "Oh, no," he said, "not in that capacity. What I need is a good bill collector."

I felt my face flush as I stammered an awkward apology, which he accepted with a smile. This little joke not only broke the ice that day, it became a standing point of humor throughout our rela-tionship in later years.

After completing my treatment on the horse and bidding farewell to Mr. Abernathy—I still wasn't comfortable addressing him as Brent at this point—I taxied the plane to the end of the

Just One More Thing, Doc

runway for take-off. The strip ran closely parallel to the main road that skirted the island. As I approached the end to make my turn, I saw an ancient pickup truck turning off the road and heading onto the runway. I had a funny feeling someone was trying to catch me, a feeling that was confirmed when the driver stopped his truck right in front of the turning plane, no more than twenty feet from the whirling propeller. A man wearing a soiled white feed cap and overalls got out. For safety, I turned off the engine as he walked around to my window, which I rolled down.

"You Doc Brown, the vet'nary?" he asked.

"Yup."

"I heard you was comin' over here and I thought while you're here I'd get ya to look at my milk cow. She ain't calved for a year and a half now. I figure her organs are out of kilter. I got a mess of young 'uns soppin' up a lot of milk and butter comin' from her. Only live a couple miles down island. I'd sure be obliged if you'd take a look." The man spoke in a long breathless stream.

"Sure," I said. "Let me park this plane out of the way and get my grips."

A few minutes later we were walking to his truck. "You'll have to get in on my side, Doc. That door ain't worked for awhile." During the drive I watched the front tires through the rusted floor-boards as we banged along.

"What's your name?" I asked.

"Erwin Emmett. My folks and past folks were all born and died on this island ever since the Pilgrims discovered it."

I hadn't realized that the Pilgrims had discovered Vinalhaven. "Is your wife from the island, too?"

"Yup. She was an Emmett afore I married her. So was my mother afore she married my father."

"Distant cousins?"

Erwin Emmett shook his head. "My mother and my wife's folks

Both Ends of the Island

are from the other side, up island, six or seven miles—a whole different bunch up that way."

I mulled that one, trying to imagine how that distance would serve as a barrier during a long winter on a sparsely populated island where snowmobiling was the main form of off-season recreation. "What do you do for a living over here, Emmett?"

"Oh, little bit of everythin'. In the summer I tend to the lawns and grounds for the summer folks. In the winter I shovel a little snow and cut a little wood, collect unemployment, and fight with the old lady."

"Yeah," I said, "winters get pretty long, I reckon."

"Uh-huh, but it's nice to have the place back when the summer people leave. I get tired a listenin' to 'em moan and groan about losing a million here and a thousand there. One rich fella I worked for had a heart attack last month on the golf course. He had one of them portable telephones strapped right to him, and 'bout every hour he was calling New York about his money," Erwin said, pausing to draw a breath. "I was luggin' his clubs that day. He'd clouted that little white ball into a manmade pond and asked me to get it out, but I told him I couldn't swim. So he waded out and fell flatter 'n a flounder. Short-circuited that little phone too, he did. He came out of there just a sputterin' and started jumpin' up and down on that telephone. Then all of a sudden he fell down cold."

"What happened then?"

"We dragged him down to the island medical center and they revived the old skinflint. He's back home already with a private nurse comin' in from New York tonight. Gawd, that fella's tighter than the bark on a elm tree. He once asked me if I wanted a pair of sneakers. I said I'd look 'em over, and you shoulda seen 'em— holes right through the toes, never mind that they didn't fit me." Erwin stopped again, shaking his head.

Just One More Thing, Doc

"So what else can you tell me about this cow?" I asked.

"Well, she's about seven years old. I raised her myself. She's had a calf every year since she was two, except for the last year and a half. I never had no trouble breedin' her. I'd wait till she had her second heat after calvin' and just lead her up island to Ben Clauson's bull. Never had no trouble getting' knocked up. Well, starting a year and a half ago she must've fallen in love with Ben's bull. She come into heat about two months after calvin', so I took her up to Ben's for a poke. But seven months later she came back into heat on me. Since then she's been in heat most of the time."

"Did you take her over to Ben's again?"

"Yeah, I been keeping her over to Ben's a couple days a week. Figure the more pokes she gets the better chance she'll have for getting with calf. One of the fellas on the island told us to change her drinkin' water, cause mine might be lackin' minerals. So I lugged her water from the neighbor's well till my back nearly broke. Didn't make a mite of difference."

This turned out to be one of several folk remedies Erwin had applied. He had also had the cow bred "on the full moon" and pointed her head downhill "so the seed won't fall out so fast." He had fed her ground-up clam and lobster shells soaked in sardine oil for a week, bred her facing southeast on a windy day, and so on. I was relieved to have these tales end when we arrived at Erwin's humble domicile. His dooryard served as a final resting place for three rusting vehicles, bedsprings, discarded clothing, broken toys, and every imaginable form of household trash. The cow's living quarters consisted of a filthy hovel standing apart from the refuse piles. Erwin walked me over to it.

After donning a plastic sleeve, I lubricated it with disinfectant soap and inserted my arm into the cow's rectum as far as my shoulder. After a couple of minutes I located and carefully manipulated both ovaries and found a four-inch cystic follicle, a frequent cause of infertility in cattle. This finding confirmed the tentative diagnosis I had made as Erwin recited the breeding history during our ride.

I withdrew my arm. "Do you know what a cyst is Erwin?"

"Not exactly," he allowed.

"Well, it's a growth, but it's not cancerous. This cow has a cyst about the size of a golf ball on one of her ovaries, and it's full of the female hormone estrogen, among other things." Erwin nodded. "The cyst is causing her to be in heat most of the time. What we have to do is to give her another kind of hormone, called chorionic gonadotropin, to start her on a regular cycle again."

"Mercy," he clucked. "How long did you have to go to school to learn that word?"

"Too long, Erwin. This hormone I'm giving her comes from pregnant mares' urine. It takes gallons of urine to get enough of the hormone to treat one cow."

"Huh. They use that same stuff on people?"

"Sure. The only difference is in the dose. It takes ten or fifteen times as much to treat a cow as it would a person. And yet they charge you two or three times more for a human dose."

"What do you think her chances are, Doc?"

"Well, with the treatment, she has about a seventy percent chance of calving again. Without it, she's beef."

"Hell, Doc. Give it right to her."

About that time one of Erwin's boys came into the shed. "Momma don't want you to forget the horse's teeth, Daddy," the boy said shyly.

"God, I almost forgot. There's just one more thing, Doc; I wanted you to check the woods horse's teeth and tell me how old you think he is. You can tell by looking at his teeth, can't you?"

"Within an hour of birth," I said, kidding. "That close enough for you, Erwin?"

"Really?"

"Naw, I was only kidding. But I can tell within a year or so, if his teeth have worn normally."

Erwin turned to the boy. "Lloyd, take some grain and run down to the pasture and fetch that horse. Doc here's in a hurry."

"Where'd you get this horse, Erwin?"

"Me and my buddy, Pearly Palmer, bought this horse from a trader on the mainland. We're makin' payments. The fella allowed he's only nine years old, but a couple of old-timers over here claim he's somewhere 'round fifteen. Pearly and me want to know the truth."

I reached into the horse's mouth, and after holding his tongue aside to view his teeth, turned to Erwin to deliver the bad news. "Hate to tell you this, Erwin, but this fella saw his twentieth birthday a couple years ago."

Erwin balled his hands into fists. "That S.O.B. of a horse jockey is gonna have to drop the price or take him back, and we ain't making no more payments till one or the other," he fumed. "Pearly's gonna bust a gasket."

"Yeah, I guess I'd feel the same way," I said. I started to wash up.

Erwin cleared his throat. "Uh, Doc," he said, "speaking of payments, I'm not too flush at the moment. Why don't you leave me a bill and your address, and I'll send it over to you when I can?"

This hardly came as a surprise. I wrote him a bill from my pad and printed out instructions about a breeding schedule for the cow on the back of a discarded soapbox I found lying in the yard. We boarded the dilapidated pickup, clattered up the road to the plane, and I managed to take off before anyone else caught up with me.

About a year later a client from Vinalhaven came to my small-animal hospital for an appointment. When she entered the exam room with her cat, she handed me a brown paper bag.

"Erwin Emmett asked me to bring this to you," she said. "There's a note inside."

I opened the bag and found two pounds of homemade butter and the note. "Doc," it said, "the cow went out of heat and she came back into it regular again, like you said. Second heat I took her up to Ben's bull like you said to do so's to avoid twins. Took her to Ben's bull just once. This butter tells you what happened—she had a corkin' smart heifer calf. My ship still ain't come in. Hope the butter will do for now."

It was all I ever got paid by Erwin, but it was damned good butter.

5

The Pork Eater

Russell didn't have a telephone, so he went across the road to his neighbor's house to call and ask me to come out and treat his sick pig. Russell lived in an old horse hovel that he had dragged home from the woods somewhere. There were very few amenities. There was neither TV nor electricity to run one; he hauled his water from a brook. Up on the ridgepole of the horse hovel hung many hams and slabs of bacon. Russell raised two pigs a year and ate only pork.

Russell was about five foot two, weighed around 270, maybe 275 pounds, and was almost as wide as he was tall. He wore rubber boots and never any socks. And he only wore the rubber boots in the winter. The other three seasons he went barefoot. He looked like he had ground-up dust and sweat in every pore of his body. His neighbor, Maynard, said that the last time Russell had a bath was when he was weeding his garden and got caught in a thunder-shower. He thought that might have been the first time Russell had had water on his body for some years.

One of his pigs had grown to 270 pounds and suddenly gotten very ill. When I arrived I took the animal's temperature and found the pig had a fever. When I checked the heart there was a swishing sound in the mitral valve. This meant that unoxygenated blood was being sent back out into the body.

The pig's skin was very blotchy. He had diamond-shaped purple areas all over his back and sides. And with these two symptoms I was able to determine that it was erysipelas, a dreaded disease of pigs that is usually fatal. Erysipelas is a bacterial infection caused by *erysipelothrix rhusiopathiae*. The bacteria get into the bloodstream and attack the valve of the heart (a condition called vegetative endocarditis), specifically the lip of the valve. This allows tissue to build up, the valve stops opening and closing the way it should, and the blood doesn't circulate properly. Eventually there is too much unoxygenated blood circulating in the body and death results.

I injected a streptomycin-penicillin combination, which is quite effective, and also left enough to inject the pig twice a day for four more days. The neighbor, Maynard, agreed to do the injecting. He had done this for his own cows many times over the years. Teaching farmers how to give injections saved me having to come back four or five days in a row when the farmer could do it just as easily. Russell was very relieved when his neighbor agreed to do the injections. He absolutely refused to have anything to do with it.

Knowing Russell to be very religious, before I left I asked him if he had been to church.

He said, "Heck yes. I was at church last night. We had a tent meeting. And some of the time was devoted to healing. Anyone with an illness or a problem could go up for healing."

"Who was the minister?"

"Well, it was Raving Ike. He got some wound up. He gets going so he's foaming at the mout', at the sides of it, running down his cheeks and chin."

"Did Raving Ike cure anyone last night?" I asked Russell.

He said, "No, but Alfred Staples's two boys, Clarence and Freddie, went up on the stage. Clarence can't talk plain, never been able to talk plain. Couldn't go to school because of it. Freddie had polio when he was little. He has been on crutches all his life. So Raving Ike got them up there on the stage and he ran up and down pounding and thrashing, cursing the devil. Finally he laid hands on both them boys and got wound up into a big frenzy. He laid his hands on their foreheads and pushed 'em back some. He said, 'You are healed, you are healed, you are healed.' Three times for each boy."

"What happened, Russell?" I asked.

He said, "Well, Raving Ike told Freddie to fro one crutch away."

"What happened?"

"Well, he was left on one crutch. Raving Ike said, 'Fro that other crutch away,' and Freddie frew the other one away."

"Then what happened?"

"He fell on his ass. He's crippled, you know."

I had to ask, "How'd he make out with Clarence and his speech?"

He said, " I can't see t'at he helped him a mite. In fact after t'at, Freddie talked like he was tongue-tied. Alfred said he is going to take 'is boys to see Oral Roberts out West to see if he couldn't help 'em."

Maynard chimed in. "Why don't you tell Alfred Staples to turn the TV on when Oral Roberts comes on and have the boys put their hands on the set during the Healing Minute, before he spends all that money to go out West?"

"That's a good idea," Russell said.

When I was out at Maynard's afterwards for different vet duties, I would sneak across the road to Russell's pig hovel and check the heart on that pig. It did recover, and it continued to gain weight—until it ended up as hams and bacon hanging from Russell's ridgepole.

6

A Longhorn

The owner of a local poultry processing plant owned a lot of land and decided that he would put it to good use by raising some beef cattle. Over a period of time he collected about a hundred and fifty head of Hereford beef cows. He went to England to purchase a bull to improve the genetics of his new herd. After a couple of years the bull, which was supposed to be hornless, began to grow horns. They grew very fast. One of them, instead of growing straight out, curled around, curving in toward his head. Eventually it pressed up against his frontal sinus bone and something had to be done about it.

I went out and looked him over and decided that I had to come up with a more effective plan than the one I'd used dehorning Killer. There was a drug that I thought would do the job and that was succinylcholine. It's not an anesthetic; it paralyzes muscles. The drug is very effective but dosage is critical—or the patient will die. (Succinylcholine has been a drug used in committing homicides. At one time it was quite undetectable; there was no test that would find it in the body. Today there is a way of detecting it and this has probably deterred would-be murderers from using this drug.)

I got my dart gun, measured out a dose, and fired the dart gun into the bull's rear leg muscle. In about twenty minutes he was on the ground, completely still. His breathing was shallow but was otherwise okay. I injected a local anesthesia into the nerves leading to his horns, and after that went into effect I sawed off the horns, also pulling the arteries that supply blood to the horns so there would be less hemorrhage. The job was over.

I waited around until I saw one foot move. After about an hour or an hour and a half (I was checking his breathing all the time), I noticed him picking up his hornless head. Slowly he regained his composure and was finally standing on his own feet after a couple of hours. He didn't have any problems such as postoperative infections and went on to service the herd for another four or five years, greatly increasing the quality of the herd and producing some very beautiful Hereford calves.

7

Bang's Disease

Back in the late 1950s, brucellosis, known as undulant fever in humans and Bang's disease in cattle, was still prevalent. People could contract the disease from cattle by drinking unpasteurized milk, so the state and federal governments paid for vets to test dairy cows for the disease every year. (In humans, brucellosis is not fatal and can be treated with antibiotics, but it is incurable and results in lifelong pain and swelling in the joints, similar to arthritis.)

The test required a blood sample to be taken from the jugular vein of cattle. Although most herds tested negative, it was not uncommon to find entire herds infected with the *brucella abortus* bacterium. When detected, testing was required for each cow every forty-five days until the disease no longer showed up within the herd. The massive doses of antibiotics required for treatment were financially out of reach for most the average farmer. Many farmers had no choice but to subject the herd to repeated testing and slaughter the infected animals, a process known as culling. Via the test-and-slaughter program, the farmer received indemnity for lost cattle. But the cost of curing an entire herd could bust a farming operation and culling compensation never truly brought equity.

Suffice it to say, it was a costly, painful, and arduous task to finally rid the state of brucellosis. The state sometimes sent its own vets to do the testing, but also hired private veterinarians like me to test cattle in our locales.

Now some cows, like a lot of people, panic at the sight of hypodermic needles—especially after getting one in the neck every forty-five days for several years running. Some cows were so upset after my visits that milk production would drop 50 percent for as long as a week after testing. (As long as the cows tested negative, farmers were allowed to sell milk, even while the herd underwent the forty-five-day test cycle.) It got so the cows could smell my presence, and just the sound of my car driving into the yard would send them into a dither. They knew right well what was about to happen. Though I always made it a point to sweet-talk them as I stroked their necks before tapping the vein, explaining that I was taking only about two teaspoons of their blood, and leaving them with about eight quarts or more, most were not appeased. The extremely nervous ones would try to climb walls, break stanchions, or lunge at me to avoid the needle.

One ill-fated herd belonged to Jules Paquette. It had tested positive and been placed under quarantine by the state for several years. (The state compensated farmers very little for the loss of income.) Jules had moved to Maine five years earlier from Quebec Province and spoke very little English. Given that I spoke no other languages, Jules had my respect for knowing any English whatsoever. He was jovial and friendly, and unlike some farmers, he cooperated with the testing program 100 percent. I always enjoyed going to his farm in the village of Jackson.

One Monday in March his herd was due for its usual forty-five-day retest. I called Jules the night before to arrange the blood test after the morning milking.

"Sure, Doc," he replied. "I'm be right here. Oh, and the quarantine sign the state person put on the barn get old and fall off. Can you bring one wit' you when you come?"

"Sorry, Jules, I can't," I said. "That has to be done by one of the state guys. But I'll call them for you and I'm sure they'll replace it. See you in the morning."

A crust of ice coated the puddles when I pulled out of the driveway that morning and headed to Jackson for my first barn call along the back roads. But as the sun rose higher, the breeze carried the scent of thawing ground. I was in a good mood.

I turned into Jules's yard, noting that his old cow barn had seen better days. A high-posted wooden structure typical of barns built in the late 1860s, it rose over a cellar for manure storage, where pigs roamed about foraging for food. In the barn above, each cow was chained by the neck to a vertical pole, and each pole was secured top and bottom to horizontal wooden two-by-fours. These primitive stanchions ran the length of the barn, holding ten cows on each side. As I well knew, these tight quarters were hazardous if your job was to collect a blood sample from the neck of each cow.

On this particular morning the cows were apprehensive as usual, and as they sniffed out my presence, a general state of agitation seemed to spread from one end of the barn to the other. Jules appeared at the barn door to greet me.

"Why don't we tackle the really nervous ones first and then maybe the rest of them won't get so riled up," I suggested

Jules nodded. "That be sense, Doc, yeah."

We were making some progress, moving along the row of swishing tails and skittish hooves; Jules held the head of each cow while I tapped the vein. Then we were interrupted by a surprise visit from Jules's brother, a priest from Quebec City, whom he hadn't seen for several years. They stood behind the cows, engaged in conversation in their native Quebeçois. I paused for the introduction, then decided to keep working down the line, having

Bang's Disease

observed that the presence of another stranger was stirring up more fear in the herd. More bovine voices joined the lowing chorus of the nervous Nellies, and the old barn was atremble as they tossed their heads, tugging and pulling at their chains. The floor started quaking, and even Jules and his long-lost brother stopped chatting as the rhythmic force got their attention.

Then it happened. With a crack like a thunderclap, the entire floor collapsed into the basement. Everything flew apart and we plunged into chaos. Timbers splintered and water pipes snapped, spewing water in all directions. I found myself in a corner of the basement, knee-deep in manure but unharmed. I looked around: I was surrounded by flailing hooves as the cows, some still chained to their poles, thrashed in panic. They were tragically tangled and piled over each other. I stared helplessly as they flopped like fish on a dock, bellowing piteously. My instinct told me that I could do nothing to help them and I feared many would strangle or suffocate under the weight of their stablemates.

By some miracle, Jules and his brother surfaced in the far corner and began picking their way through the pile of entangled cows. The priest chanted rapid-fire Hail Marys as he jumped about, dodging the hooves and debris, following Jules, who was a few steps ahead of him. The two men made their way to the outside wall, and edged along it to the only window, which was set about three feet above the cellar floor. They waved for me to join them, then scrambled through the opening to safety.

I shook off the horror of the situation and started to move forward, but found myself hedged in by a sea of flailing cows about twenty feet from the window. An old timber groaned and shifted over my head, raining down a century's worth of hay chaff, insect husks, and desiccated manure. The fear of another piece of floor crashing down on my head propelled me through the morass. My legs and body were pounded, trampled, and squeezed as I crawled under and over the bellies and backs of cows. At last I squeezed out of the window, exhausted. Jules and the priest were hunkered by the opening, and each of them grabbed one of my arms and yanked me the rest of the way out.

"You be okay, Doc?" Jules asked.

"Yeah, I guess so," I answered. "How're you guys doing? Get your bolt cutters, Jules."

"We be okay, Doc," Jules said. "Pretty good. That was some near for comfort. Three or two time I thought we all be gone. But them cows, sacre bleu! What we do now?"

I glanced over at the priest. He had set to praying again in his new tattered black suit. His starched white collar was spotted with manure. Barked and bleeding knuckles clutched a rosary. I turned back to his more practical brother.

"Jules," I cried, "get your chai saw and widen out that cellar window. Maybe we can save some of 'em."

Jules tore off to the shed and soon returned with the saw, bolt cutters, and a hacksaw. He slashed through the wooden wall and it came down like a loading ramp. Some of the cows that had worked their way out of their chains limped and trotted out of the opening. Jules hollered to his brother to lead them into the paddock, and the priest, to his credit, jumped to the task.

But more than a dozen animals were still trapped under the debris. By now they were too exhausted to thrash. With more space freed up, Jules and I worked our way through the rubble cutting their neck chains and freeing the survivors. We were amazed to find that these animals had somehow survived serious injury, except for a few that had suffered deep cuts. We herded them into a paddock, and I made the rounds, checking them all and stitching up some of the wounded. In the end, we counted no dead cows. It was remarkable that they all were alive and in reasonably good shape.

"I bet you don't plan to do this while you're out here, Doc," Jules said, a smile stealing over his face.

"No, but with this job, I never know, Jules."

"I gots a pretty darn mess here my hand," he said, the smile fading as he gazed over at the barn.

During the disaster Jules's wife had called the fire department and shut off the water to the barn. Neighbors started arriving. After surveying the damage, they formed a huddle around Jules and his brother. While I collected what I could find of my gear, I overheard them making plans to chip in and help Jules repair the wrecked barn.

I told Jules that I'd phone or drop by soon to check on the injured cows. I also said that there would be no charge for my services that day or for any future attention to the injured cattle. Bruised and tired I got in my car and drove to the next farm call.

A few days later, as I was driving by on the way to a neighbor's farm, I decided to see how Jules's cows were coming along. As I pulled into his dooryard, I noted some new wood siding had been put on the barn. Jules poked his head out from under the hood of his tractor when he heard my car and broke into a broad grin, waving a greeting.

"How's it going, Jules?" I asked, walking over to him.

"Hey, Doc," he said, wiping tractor grease from his big callused hands. "Everything okay. All my neighbor help fix the barn. About twelve o'clock midnight that night we finish. Then we do the milking until half past tree tirty. I don't get much milk though."

"Well, why don't we wait a week or so to test the rest of the herd?" I suggested. "That will give them a chance to settle down. I can take out the stitches at the same time."

"That be good idea," he agreed. "Oh, Doc, while you be here, have you call up the state man about the quarantine sign?"

"Sorry," I said, "I totally forgot, but I'll call first thing tomorrow. By the way, is your brother still here?"

"Oh, no," he said, laughing. "He be here only tree or two day. He be plenty upset with me. I smoke too much, drink too much, eat too much. Then I say 'for Christ sake.' That do it. He gone to Quebec right then."

I laughed, we shook hands, and I proceeded on my way.

Another week passed, and I returned to Jules's farm as planned. An unfamiliar car was parked in the yard. When Jules came out of the house to greet me, he was far from the cheerful man I was accustomed to seeing.

"I got plenty trouble, Doc," he said. "Everybody round here treat me like two-week-old eggs. I'm go to the store and the woman there say stay away from buying grocery. The school call and say my four kid cannot go there no more. They send paper home wit' 'em, but me or the wife don't read no English, and the kid, they too small for big words. Maybe you can tell me."

"Is someone visiting?" I asked as we walked to the house.

"That newspaper lady in there, talking to my wife," he said. "We can't tell what she want."

I followed Jules into the kitchen. Sitting at the kitchen table were Cecile Paquette looking baffled and distressed, and Alma Beckett, the village "news correspondent."

Maine's small communities traditionally have had such reporters, whose job it is to call on neighbors and write up a weekly column about local happenings. Alma Beckett reported the newsy bits from three towns in a seven-day diary format, featuring items about so-and-so "motoring to Bangor on a Sunday," or "visiting with Henry and Shirlene Beckett and little Orville." The visit might include a detailed description of a meal. I recalled that last week's column had featured something along the lines of "a lovely dinner was served of roast pork, mashed potatoes, fresh garden peas, Hubbard squash, fresh strawberries, and homemade whipped cream." A big event like a grange supper was reported as breathlessly as a horse race.

I decided to lob one into Alma's court. "What's new?"

"Well, I was just talking to Cecile about what's been going on around here," she said, her eyes glistening like a ravenous animal's.

"You mean the collapse of the barn floor last week?" I asked. "I thought that was old news." Her lips puckered slightly, and she narrowed her eyes.

"The news deadline closed the morning of the incident, so it will be in next week's paper," Alma informed me. She audibly sniffed.

"Well, let's hear what you got," I said, pulling up a chair at the table. Emboldened, Jules joined me. Cecile shot him a worried look.

Clearing her throat, Alma began to read: "Saturday morning Jules Paquette lost his barn floor, dropping cows into his barn cellar. Some of them required medical attention by Dr. Brown, the veterinary from Belfast." Here she paused for dramatic effect. "The Paquette farm had been quarantined by the state due to a serious disease that is threatening the entire town and even the state. The disease is called undulant fever. There is no cure for it."

I could feel Jules's eyes boring into the side of my head, but I stared straight ahead at Alma, who was also watching my reaction. "Go on," I said.

"Mr. Bussie Beckett and myself motored over last Tuesday and saw firsthand the quarantine sign hanging on the front door." Alma didn't need to inform her readers that Bussie, her husband, was the town health inspector.

Jules and Cecile looked at each other, aghast, and Cecile rushed to the front door, which was so little used that she had to remove three cardboard boxes full of junk of open it. Down Easters seldom use the formal front door; guests and visitors enter through

Just One More Thing, Doc

a friendly side door. She returned moments later holding a yellow and black sign.

"Well," I said, smiling politely. "It looks like the state man came after all—and hung the sign on the wrong door. Jules, where's that note you wanted me to read?"

Jules spoke to Cecile in French, and she went to a drawer to fetch a handwritten note. I took it from her and read aloud, "Dear Mr. and Mrs. Paquette: Until your quarantine is over, your children should be kept home. A letter from the state health officer will be required before they will be readmitted to class." It was signed by the elementary school principal.

Jules grasped the gist of it and immediately communicated to Cecile in French. A light went on in her face. Still standing, she spoke back to Jules, and he turned to Alma and me. "Doc," he pleaded. "tell Mrs. Beckett here that she need to change what she write."

Alma's face sagged. "Dr. Brown, is that true?"

"Afraid so," I said. "Brucellosis affects cattle, pigs, sheep, goats, and humans, and Jules has been cooperating with the state testing program for almost two years. People can catch it only if they drink unpasteurized milk from an animal carrying the disease or from carelessly handling an aborted fetus from an infected cow. This isn't news to me."

I had all I could do not to gloat as Alma started gathering up her things. She thanked the Paquettes for their time and wished them a rather tart "good day."

As soon as he heard Alma's car start, Jules tipped back his head and howled with laughter. I joined him, and eventually, even Cecile caught the drift and joined in.

Three months later, Jules Paquette's herd finally tested negative. The state and federal courts gave Jules a generous stipend for the loss of milking cows to brucellosis and for the loss of milk production over several years, and yes, they also paid for the physical damage to his cow barn!

8

Harry Called

One afternoon Harry called to say that he had four cows off their feed and could I stop by, at my convenience, to take a look at them and tell him what was wrong? I acknowledged I would, but it probably wouldn't be until that evening.

When Harry showed me the four cows, all in a row, the first thing I noticed was that they were all dehydrated. Looking around I saw discolored feces that were very hard. I walked up between the first two cows and looked into their shared water dish. The cows got water by pressing on a lever in the dish with their noses. It wasn't working. I went up between cows three and four and they had a similar problem.

Harry said, "Dammit! I had to pay you to come out here to show me how stupid I am."

I said, "Pay it no mind, Harry. I see this all the time." We talked for a few minutes. It would be a simple matter to fix the water system and restore the health of the cows.

Before I was able to get off the property, Harry caught up with me. "Just one more thing, Doc. My hired man Tink said the bull hasn't urinated for days. Tink cleans out his bed every day and says it's been dry as a bone."

I went up behind the bull, stood there, and watched him. He

was very uneasy, treading all the time, moaning and groaning with every breath. I went to my car and got a sterile sleeve for an exam.

The bull's bladder was distended many times its normal size and rock hard. He was in tremendous pain. There was a marble-sized bladder stone lodged in his urethra, which is the tube—in man and beast—that carries urine from the bladder to its outside destination.

I proceeded to give the bull a spinal anesthetic, which took him out of pain and relaxed his penis. I went to my car and fetched out a three-foot catheter and some petroleum jelly. I inserted it into the end of the penis and then put on another sleeve. Going back into the pelvis, I had Harry push gently against the catheter until I could feel it come up against the stone. At that point I told Harry to give it a couple of short, sharp jabs. He did, and then, more gently, pushed it into the bladder itself. Slowly but surely the stone dropped back into the bladder. At the same time urine started to flood out of the catheter. Before it was over, a gallon or a gallon and a half of fluid had spilled onto the floor. I could feel the bull relax immediately. His treading and moaning stopped, and he was once again feeling normal.

I gave him a long-acting antibiotic called bi-cillin to fight any infections that might crop up in the urethra or bladder. I also gave him a dose of long-acting estrogen, because I had noticed that his prostate was quite enlarged. I told Harry that I would check the bull's prostate again the next time I was out this way. I did and the results were very good. He was a working bull again.

I washed up my gear, disinfected my boot,s and was about to go when I heard my two-way radio say, "Two Four Two. Come in please." It was my mother. She said that Carroll Fowler from Lincolnville called to say that he had a cow that had been trying to calve all day. It needed my help. So I was off to Moody Mountain, to Carroll Fowler's little farm on the side of the hill.

To get to Carroll's farm, the shortest route was to go across Muzzy Ridge Road. This was the road that went up and over Moody Mountain. The time of year meant the frost was about out. I decided to risk it, believing that I could make it across. From this shortcut it was an easy distance down the mountain to Carroll's farm. I would save seven miles over the smoother and more level alternative of the tarred road that went around the mountain.

I arrived and about a half-hour later delivered a very healthy seventy-five-pound heifer calf. That made Carroll's day because it was out of one of his best cows. She was unable to deliver naturally because the head and neck of the calf had been extended severely toward the flank of the mother. Whereas my arms were longer than Carroll's, I had the advantage I needed to deliver the calf. After several while-you're-here-Doc pregnancy checks and vaccinating a handful of six-month-old heifers against brucellosis, I was off for the next farm visit.

While I had been at Carroll's farm there had been a terrific spring thundershower and it rained buckets, a torrential downpour. Now I had a decision. How to get back? Do I go back up Muzzy Ridge Road on Moody Mountain or go around, driving an extra seven miles? Being a gambler, of course I decided to go over the mountain. This turned out to be a terrific mistake, as you are about to find out.

When I came to the Ridge Road I turned left and headed up over the mountain. I chose the right side of the road as it seemed to give more traction. I reached the top of the mountain and headed across for about a mile on Muzzy Ridge Road, which was now nothing but a muddy surface. Rain had gotten into it, and it was a mess. I slipped sideways and almost became mired a couple of times, but fate was good to me and I kept moving ahead. I was becoming more confident that I could make it.

A deer came out into the road and stood motionless about fifty yards in front of my car. I blew my horn but the deer remained still. I inched ahead and as I did I felt the car settling. It was an eerie feeling. Down it went right up to the axles of the vehicle. I was the victim of a giant sinkhole. What was left of the frost was no more. I knew immediately that I was helpless.

I rolled the driver's window down and climbed out through the window. I slogged down the muddy road to a farmer I knew about a half-mile away.

Howard was in the yard and after I explained my predicament, he fetched a couple of chains and started the largest tractor that he had. We climbed on and headed for my sunken car. When Howard looked it over he seemed shocked.

"This is the worst stuck car I've ever seen," he said.

He handed me the end of a chain and told me to wrap it around the bumper anchor, which I did. I handed him the other end of the chain. He slipped it onto the housing of his tractor. He tied the chain to the strongest position on his tractor, then told me to stand back in case the chain snapped.

The chain became taut but the car didn't move an inch. The tractor *was* able to remove the front bumper from my car, though.

"Sorry about that," Howard apologized.

He suggested we try to pull it backwards as it might lift some of the rear suction off the car. I hooked the chain onto the two rear bumper anchors of the frame. Again Howard put the end of the chain on his tractor housing. He went very slowly. The car didn't move an inch. We got the same result. The rear bumper was torn from the car and Howard apologized again.

"Only a bulldozer is going to get you out," he said. "Unless we can break the suction you're going to stay stuck."

We went down to his neighbor, whom I've known for years, and explained to Clarence what the situation was.

Clarence said, "You know better than to go down Muzzy Ridge

Road this time of year, Doc."

"I've been doing it for years, Clare. But I certainly shouldn't have, today. When you see it you'll know why."

Clare jumped onto his Caterpillar 'dozer. Howard and I got on also and we set off at a snail's pace down the Muzzy Ridge Road to my imprisoned car. When we reached the car, Howard and Clare walked around it to make a plan.

I was already covered in mud from head to foot, so I went under the rear of the car, and with what little room I could make, attached the chain. Clare wrapped the other end around the bucket of his bulldozer, raised the bucket, and voilà, the car's rear end came out of the mire.

We used a big log to prop up the freed part of the car and repeated the whole procedure on the front end of the car. Then Clare pulled the car forward, and we were some relieved to see it move. Hallelujah!

We started the slow crawl back to Howard's place. When we reached his milkroom and Clare shut off the bulldozer, I excused myself, grabbed a change of clothes from my car, stripped to the waist in the milkroom, and proceeded to have a cold shower to remove some of the mud. I also sprayed the car, but it still looked like it had been through a California mudslide.

I started up my car, said my good-byes, and was thanking Howard profusely when Clare came over and said, "While you're here, Doc, I've got three cows that need blood sugar bad."

I said, "Okay, Clare. I'll stop and meet you down there."

I treated his three cows and was leaving when Clare said, "How much do I owe you, Doc?"

I said, "You don't owe me anything, Clare. In fact, I owe you. I want to tell you that you and Howard aren't going to receive a vet bill for a year." And off I went to the four or five farms I still had yet to visit.

Harry Called

I went about finishing my barn rounds, got back to the office at four in the morning, and checked the surgical cases and the rest of the patients. I went home and had a lovely meal out of the warming oven. Then I sat in the armchair in the living room to write down what I had done and where I had been that evening on barn rounds. Later I staggered upstairs to try to get a couple of hours of sleep, at least, before the next farmer called after finding something wrong when he got to his barn in the morning.

Never again did I take a chance on Muzzy Ridge Road on Moody Mountain during the spring of the year.

9

Butter? No, Thanks

I picked up the phone. The voice on the other end said, "Is this Dr. Brown?"

I said, "Yes."

"I'm Ed Scott on the old Merrithew Farm in Prospect. Got a cow with a bad skin humor here. It's not an emergency."

"I'll come over tomorrow evening," I informed him.

I drove into the yard of a small side-of-the-hill farm. At the peak of the ol, necrotic barn, etched into a weathered board, were the barely discernible numbers "1788." Most of the barn had fallen down and one half of the roof was held together only by the cedar shingles. The shed was precariously swinging by its attachment to the old house, and the house had open holes in the roof that were covered with tarps. The porch was hanging by big hay-strap ropes half the length of it. Under the jury-rigged porch roof were two chairs suspended by ropes.

One of the chairs held up, tenuously, one of the most obese women I had ever seen. As I approached her I noticed she was reading an old *Hustler* magazine. She was puffing hard on a cigarette and after taking a deep breath, fell into a coughing fit. After she regained her breath she asked, "Are you veterinary Brown?"

"Yes," I replied.

"Ed's been expecting you. One of his cows has a skin humor. He wants to try to stop it before the rest of the cows get infected. Just follow this side of the old barn and be sure to stay this side of the manure piles."

I made it to the end of the old barn by balancing myself against the barn until I came to a doorless tie-up. It contained the milking cows.

There was a man hand-milking a cow while sitting on his tree-stump milk stool. He looked up at me and said, "My name is Ed." He was a very small man, about five feet tall and weighing no more than 120 pounds. He had a full beard crusted around his mouth by chewing tobacco, and I saw him frequently spit on the inside of his ten fingers as he milked. He wore only bib overalls and no shoes. On his head he wore an old WWI army hat, the front folded backwards so it pressed up against his forehead. The front flap of the hat was dark brown from years of contact with a cow's flank. The milk itself was tobacco brown from his beard drippings falling into the pail.

Ed stood up and said, " I lease this old farm from the folks who inherited it. They claim they are the eighth generation to own it. I hope to build up the herd so I can ship my milk out to a big dairy like Hood in Boston. Right now I'm making butter and selling it to the local grocery stores."

Then he pointed out the infected cow, which he really didn't have to because the "skin humor" was so obvious. From years of clinical experience I recognized it immediately as ringworm.

He showed me spots on other cows where the fungus had started to get to them. I excused myself and started out to the car to get some medication.

"Can I give you a hand, Doc?"

"No, thanks, Ed."

Just after I'd arrived there had been a heavy thundershower. It produced a torrential downpour, making the dooryard a quagmire. Steam was rising off the mud, and ducks and chickens were pecking away at the earthworms and other insects driven to the surface by the deluge. I had a time of it getting to my car.

I grabbed the medication and carefully made my way back to the so-called barn. I gave the infected cows a heavy dose of vitamin A and oil (a suppository form of vitamin A that lasts much longer than the aqueous solution), and I gave Ed an iodine-based shampoo to use on them.

Ed picked up two pails of milk and said, "Follow me." He hobbled back, guided by the side of the barn and the path though the manure, to the old kitchen, where he set the two pails of milk on the floor. About that time his six children appeared from the room off the kitchen that had straw mattresses spread around. The children were obviously no more than a year apart one from another. They were very polite and disciplined.

A large Walker hound by the stove rose to his feet. Duke was Ed's favorite dog. He walked over to one pail of milk, lifted a leg, and proceeded to urinate. Though barefooted, Ed kicked him lightly in the ribs saying, "Duke, you old S.O.B. Now I've got to strain that milk!"

Ed's wife appeared from the dilapidated porch and said, "Ed, we gotta strain that milk. There must be a hundred dead flies in there. Flies don't look very good in butter."

Ed said, "Woman, you got money to pay the vet?"

"Hell, no. I sent the last of our money to buy two new subscriptions to magazines yesterday. Maybe he'll take his pay in butter, Ed."

I thought quickly and said, "Thanks, anyway, but my wife doesn't use butter in our house."

Before leaving I advised Ed that there would soon be a new law that required testing cows every six months for brucellosis and tuberculosis. This would be mandatory for all cows whose milk or milk products would be sold to the public unpasteurized. (In my day, milk was consumed in the same state as when it left the cow. We survived, although our dad lost a lot of cows to brucellosis.)

Ed said, "I'll be damned if I get my cows tested every six months. I'll sell 'em first."

I got into my car to leave and Ed rapped on my window as I was jockeying around to get out of his yard. I hit my brakes, then rolled down the window.

Ed said, "Just one more thing, Doc. I intended for ya to take a look at my bitch Walker hound. She must have something plugged up. All of her tears run down her cheek, run down the corner of her eye. Must be something wrong."

I went and took a quick look at her, and found that she had a plugged naso-lacrimal duct—the little tube that allows excess tears in the corner of one's eye to drain into one's nose.

I always carried a few small catheters and I went and got one. I gave her a tranquilizer, anesthetized the eye with opthaine, and opened that plugged duct.

"If it bothers her again, let me know," I told Ed. I never heard about it again so I assumed things went well.

But Ed did end up selling all his cows.

10

The Stallion and the Mercedes

Police were blocking off streets, fire trucks were blocking off streets, people were out on the sidewalks, sirens were going off everywhere. Why? It all started when a Bangor patholo-gist asked if I could castrate his ten-year-old Arabian stallion.

He had Arabian show horses for his daughter Hillary, and this particular horse was getting to be too much for her to handle. The stallion got away from her at the last show and went after an Arabian mare from Massachusetts.

"I should have sent them a bill for stud fees," the doctor quipped.

The day I drove up to Bangor turned out to be warm, so I decided to operate outdoors in the paddock. It contained an acre of land, was enclosed by a high wooden fence, and the stallion was used to the paddock as his exercise yard. I asked to have an expe-rienced horseman to help with the anesthesia, and with getting the horse down and then back up. The experienced horseman didn't show up.

I was anxious to get started and got the doctor to agree to stand in for the no-show. There was another gentleman present and he also agreed to help out.

I carefully explained to them the entire procedure so that they could play their parts without fail. The doctor brought the stallion out from his stall and led him into the paddock. The horse was a frisky lad, and he reared up and neighed a couple of times. I quickly gave him an intravenous sedative injection to expedite the anesthesia, which would be coming up shortly. This put him in a mild state of lethargy, and in about fifteen minutes I gave him an intravenous injection of sodium pentothal. He went down calmly and comfortably, and the surgery went well.

He was a well-endowed stallion so I made sure to put good ligatures on the spermatic cord to keep bleeding at a minimum. While we were waiting for the patient to recover, the doctor mentioned that he had just bought the car that was sitting in the white pea-rock driveway. It was a Mercedes convertible, a beautiful car—jet black, with a white canvas top.

The plan was to have the doctor and his friend on either side of the leads coming off the horse's halter. I would control the horse from the rear by using his tail as a guide to help him balance once he reached his feet. I said that under no circumstances should they let him out of the paddock. "We've got an acre here, and that's plenty of room for his recovery area. Also, it's his natural environment."

Pretty soon he was both physically and mentally conscious. Things were going according to plan. Soon he was on his feet, though very wobbly, like a drunk. We managed to keep him on his feet as we walked him around the paddock. It wasn't very long before he was fully alert. To prove it, he suddenly bolted from us, making straight for the closed paddock gate. He cleared the five-foot gate by a foot.

He was soon distracted by lush lawn and started grazing. I sent the doctor for a pail of grain, a horse's first choice for food. He returned and called to the patient by name, "Larri!" The horse had been named for Lawrence of Arabia.

Instead of holding the pail up for Larri's convenience (and

making it easier to grab the halter leads), the doctor made the mistake of pouring the grain out on the ground. The second the doctor reached for the leads, Larri bolted out of reach. It was a cat-and-mouse game now.

As he was devouring the last of the grain, I crept up on him from behind, made a split-second lunge, grabbed a lead with both hands, and hung on tightly. But Larri bolted away again, pulling the leather strap from my hands with such force that it burned my hands in several places.

Then he decided to head south on Ohio Street, one of Bangor's longest streets.

The doctor called the police and ran for his new Mercedes convertible. "Get in, Doc," he said to me. We proceeded to follow Larri down to the end of Ohio Street, which the police had blocked off with a fire truck. When Larri came to it he veered off at a ninety-degree angle to the right and ended up on Union Street.

He didn't like the police cars on that street, eventually found his way back to Ohio Street, and from there headed toward home.

We were waiting for him, parked in the doctor's new Mercedes, horizontal to the mouth of the yard. We were soon joined by two police cars which also parked horizontally, at each end of the Mercedes, so that we had the street pretty well blocked off. We got out of the doctor's car and positioned ourselves to try to flag Larri into his dooryard or at least onto his home territory.

We saw Larri coming down Ohio Street straight towards us at a fast gallop. About twenty yards away from the parked cars he veered suddenly to the right onto the lawn of his home. Using more grain as bait, we coaxed him into his box stall inside the stable after about twenty minutes.

The doctor's helper went about giving the horse some fresh-cut timothy hay. We were standing outside, enjoying the calm, when we heard a tremendous crash, followed by the sound of metal and glass landing on the street. We hastened toward the source of the noise.

It seems one of the policemen had received an emergency call and had jumped into his vehicle. He accidentally hit reverse with his car at full throttle and it shot backwards into the front of the doctor's new Mercedes convertible. Suffice it to say, the damage was considerable. The Ford police cruiser didn't fare much better.

The doctor sputtered something to the effect that the salesman had told him the Mercedes was as strong as a tank. He thought about taking a picture and showing it to the salesman, just to see what he had to say.

The doctor and the policeman went into the house to fill out insurance paperwork, and I did a final check on the patient. I wanted to make sure that there was no post-surgical bleeding. All the running around wasn't normal post-op recovery, but my sutures had held well.

I gave the doctor instructions on how to care for the patient during his recovery and was loading my gear and instruments into my car when he said, "Just one more thing, Doc. Would you take a quick look at my boxer's mouth? He has growths on his gingiva. Looks like hyperplasia, but they're getting larger over time."

My examination revealed a problem seen in some boxers. Gingival hyperplasia, in advanced cases, causes little growths of tissue that become larger, start to bleed, and can cause bigger problems down the road. I explained to the doctor that he had better have his vet check it out on his next visit.

He said, "No, you're our vet now. I've observed you carefully today, Dr. Brown, and I prefer to have you for our veterinarian for all our animals. I never realized what a large-animal veterinarian goes through. It's been an education for me!"

They brought the dog in for surgery and he did fine. I had a long-standing relationship with the doctor and his family. Their daughter Hillary took pre-vet at the University of Maine at Orono and then applied to vet school. I was happy to write her a recommendation, having gotten to know her well over the years. She got her VMD from the University of Pennsylvania and became an equine veterinarian.

11

Anthrax: A Sure Killer

Allen Jones, dairy farmer, went out to get his cows in for milking from the pasture at the end of the day. He found his prized show cow dead in the pasture. He was very upset when he called me on the phone.

"Could you come out and find out what happened?" he asked.

"I'll be out in a couple of hours, Allen."

When I arrived he took me right out to where the dead cow was. One thing stuck out more than anything else. She had blood coming from every orifice in her body—nostrils, anus, and ears, everywhere.

"What do you suppose happened to her, Doc?" Allen asked. "She was perfectly fine when I turned her out this morning. She gave her usual amount of milk, she hasn't been off feed, and she hasn't acted a mite sick, Doc."

"Allen, there are many reasons for sudden death. Did you have a thundershower here today? No. Other things come to mind—lead poisoning; plant poisoning like bracken fern; drowning."

We did a thorough search of the farm, especially the pasture, and none of the life-threatening things I had thought of appeared to be present. It had to be something that caused massive hemorrhage. After walking over the entire pasture, two things came to mind.

Years ago a man named Scofield in Canada went out on a call to see a farmer. He was with the vet school in Guellph, Canada, and what he found were dead cows in a field of sweet clover. Ten out of twenty in the herd were dead. The vet took samples of the sweet clover back to the college. The lab there extracted coumidin from the plant. The drug coumidin is used in human and animal medicine to prevent blood from clotting—it's a blood-thinner. That explained why the Canadian cows had hemorrhaged to death.

But there was no sweet clover present at Allen's farm.

Allen asked, "Are you going to cut her open, Doc?"

I said, "Well, no. I just recalled what a professor of bacteriology told me once. If you cut them open it will just expose the bacteria that might be in there, putting healthy animals at risk from the bacteria spores."

Once I said that, I knew I had the diagnosis. My second thought had been something that I hoped we wouldn't get to— anthrax. So I wasn't going to do a postmortem.

"I'm just going to take a swab. There are some sophisticated laboratory tests for anthrax, but there is also a barnyard test. It works, sometimes."

I took a stick, put a swab on it, and swabbed the cow's bloody nose. Once the blood had saturated the swab I stuck it in one of my metal lab tubes and took this back to my office.

At the office I placed it on the windowsill in the sun so it would dry out. After it had dried thoroughly, I made three microscope slide smears. The reason for drying out the swab is to eliminate other bacteria, viruses, and contaminants. Only the spores of the anthrax would remain intact, theoretically.

I numbered the slides 1, 2, and 3. Examining them under the microscope I saw nothing on slide 1. I went over slide 2 with a fine-toothed comb and it also produced nothing, I was hesitant about checking the third slide because statistically, chances were small, but I looked and there it was. It was a perfect example of a vegetative anthrax spore.

I called Allen and told him we had a positive test for anthrax in the show cow.

"What can we do?" he asked.

I said, "If you really want to, we can vaccinate the rest of the herd with anthrax vaccine. I don't have any but I can get it overnight."

"Go ahead and order it, Doc, if that's what we've got to do."

I got on the phone with a drug company that I did business with and ordered enough to vaccinate the rest of his cattle. I told Allen to bury the cow as soon as possible and to be sure to use a lot of lime so that predators wouldn't show up and spread the spores. I also cautioned him to spread lime around the area where the cow had lain all day. Anthrax spores when inhaled cause inhalation anthrax, which is highly fatal.

Anthrax is a reportable disease, so I immediately called the state veterinarian in Augusta. He asked if he could come over and look at the slide. I said, "Anytime," and he said he was on his way.

He verified what I saw. Then he asked directions to the Joneses' farm, where he told Allen that the place would have to be quarantined until further notice. The yellow quarantine signs went up: "ANTHRAX! KEEP OUT!"

The vaccine came the next day and I went out to Allen's farm that evening. We vaccinated every cloven-hoofed animal there, all the cattle. The case that I diagnosed was classified as an isolated sporadic event, and Allen went on to continue dairying for years.

Humans who are in contact with animals, particularly slaughterhouse workers, bonemeal producers, fur skinners of wild animals, and wool sorters, are at risk for anthrax every day. The hair from alpacas and llamas is also a risky source of infection. Anyone at risk should be vaccinated against anthrax as a safeguard.

Anthrax is found in two forms, both treatable with a combination of antibiotics and vaccine. There is more success with cutaneous anthrax than with inhalation anthrax after exposure.

Cutaneous anthrax is usually contracted through openings in the skin, as in cuts and sores. It results in swelling and edema in the limb or the part of the body that is affected. It has a special affinity for lymph nodes that are trying to fight off infection as a response by the infected person's immune system. This form is more prevalent in slaughter shops where workers frequently nick themselves while killing the animals.

Inhalation anthrax is the most lethal form. It enters via the lungs, then it seeks out the lymph nodes and destroys them. Septicemia sets in next, followed by death, usually in two to three days. One can see that this bacterium is bent on destroying the immune system of its victim as quickly as possible, making it one of the most feared diseases on the planet.

12

A Sheep Story Times Three

One day I was very busy in the hospital when Ken C. called and said that one of his ewes had been in labor too long, and it was her first birth. I had to tell Ken that I was in the middle of an extensive surgery and would come as soon as was possible.

Ken was a wonderful man who was basically a poultry farmer but also had about sixty head of sheep, which he gave the very best care. They each had a name and were like children to him. He was the best shepherd I ever knew.

I arrived and my examination of the expectant mother in labor resulted in an unusual dystocia—Perrin's abnormal positioning in the uterus of the fetus, orfetuses in this case. Twins are a common event in sheep. So after lubricating the birth canal and my hand and fingers and rubber gloves, I followed the front legs back, one by one, until I got to their little heads and repositioned them into the proper birthing position. The twins were delivered alive. I got them breathing normally and went back in the uterus to attempt to retrieve the afterbirth, but I immediately hit an obstacle. It was another head of a lamb. I had found the other part of the puzzle and promptly delivered a healthy, extra-large male lamb.

I took lots of time with him, as he was the last one. I got him into the birth canal and his mother strained. Her strong labor contractions seemed to remove the mucus from the lungs of the lamb as its ribcage pushed through the canal. This is a critical stage of birth, which squeezes the thick, viscous fluid out of the newborn lungs. This fluid has filled the creature's lungs throughout gestation. The sooner the fluid comes out, the better for the animal's respiration. It always seems like a miracle when the umbilical cord is severed and the lungs begin working immediately. Breathing heralds the beginning of life.

Ken was very pleased that there were two females and the last one was a male. They all soon gained their feet and suckled their mother's first milk. Triplets aren't common in sheep, so usually you have to choose one and raise it on a bottle. Ken picked the male, raising him on a bottle as he had for many orphaned lambs before.

Dystocias—abnormal birth positions—are the biggest cause of delayed births in all vertebrates. I often think how sad it is that deer and other wild animals end up dead without help. I can't recall any part of my practice being more rewarding and satisfying than to correct a fetus that couldn't enter the world, and be able to witness the start of a new life.

13

A Trip To Boston

F rank was a good neighbor and well liked. He operated a small farm in Winterport, Maine, about fifteen miles north of Belfast. He kept about thirty milking cows but really made his money with his apple orchard. It had been nurtured over the years into a very profitable venture.

One day Frank called me in to take care of a sick cow. While I was there the usually quiet man started talking excitedly about his recent trip to Boston as the president of Maine's Pomological Society that year. As president he received an all-expense-paid trip to the New England Pomological Society's meeting. It was held at least once a year, back in the 1950s anyway.

"Geez, that was quite a trip, Doc. I'm sixty-three years old and I've never been out of the state of Maine before. I didn't have a reservation but the president from the year before said that I could stay at the Parker House where the meeting was being held. It's a big hotel and they would be sure to have a room.

"I took the train from Bangor to Boston. It was quite a ride. When I got in Boston, I got a taxicab ride to the Parker House. During the ride I could see the tall buildings all around me but not the tops of them. I never see such a sight in my life. Heard about Boston all my life but never realized what it was really like.

"The cabdriver got me safely to the Parker House and he dropped me off. I walked into the lobby and walked over to the sign-in desk. I rang the little bell and a man came out and explained to me that they didn't have a single room available. The man said they had over nine hundred rooms but they were all filled, since there were three conventions going on at once there over the next few days—the place was jammed. But he told me not to despair, that people come and go, and cancellations were possible. If I was patient and checked in every hour, there might be a change. He said he would do the best he could to get me in.

"I thanked him and he told me while I was waiting, I should use the dining facilities, then check in with him again. I took his advice, since I was pretty hungry. I went into the dining room; it was a beautiful, large room. I was seated by a waiter in a tuxedo-type uniform. He had a black bow tie and a white shirt and tuxedo trousers, that sort of thing. It was most impressive.

"The waiter said, 'Sir, I would like to offer you our menu, but first I would suggest you begin with our soup du jour.'

"I said that I had never heard of soup du jour. I guess that he understood what I was talking about.

"He said, 'That means soup of the day, sir. Here at the Parker House that means clam chowder, for which we are well known. People come from all over the country to try our signature soup.' He gave me quite a sales pitch about that clam chowder, but I don't like clam chowder. He finally gave up on that and I ordered some beans and hot dogs. I finished it off with some apple pie with ice cream on top.

"I left the dining room and went back out to the front desk where I found the same gentleman that I had spoken with before. He said, 'Mister, you are just in luck. One of our clients has just died on the ninth floor. He has been here for years and he was very ill, with a nurse twenty-four hours a day. He has passed away and been removed, and the room has been cleaned and sterilized. It's the only room we've got now or probably will have.' Being desperate and because it was getting quite late, I said, 'I'll take it.'

"A boy in a red hat came and took my boxful of clothes, which my wife had carefully packed. He got me to the elevator and we rode up nine floors. We walked down a long, long hall until he stopped and opened a door. He went into the room ahead of me, opened the curtains, and told me that if I left my shoes outside they would shine them. There would also be a newspaper outside of the door in the morning. Then he left.

"I could see half of Boston as I stood looking out those beautiful windows. Wow! I took my shoes off and walked over those wonderful Persian rugs till I almost wore my socks out. The bathroom was huge. It was very exciting to see that city all lit up. I still wondered why that waiter down there wanted me to try that damn clam chowder. It kept crossing my mind why they kept at you so. He was so insistent I almost gave in and ate the damn stuff.

"I stayed up late 'cause it was a new experience. Around midnight I lay down in bed and pulled the blanket up over me and started to get sleepy even though I was still very excited. I must have fallen asleep 'cause the next thing I knew, I heard the latch on the door slam a little bit and I saw a person coming through the door in a white uniform. She looked like a nurse. She had a cap with a black stripe on it. I pulled the blanket up over my face and pretended to be dead asleep. She came over to the bed and rolled me over, gave me a high enema, and left. I was quite shaken but I wasn't hurt.

"I went to the meeting the next day and it was marvelous. A great big conference room, they fed ya little sandwiches and olives and pickles and quite a display of food. They called it lunch. I called it an eating orgy.

"We had a great meeting and I got to present a paper that I had written on grafting certain varieties of apple trees. It was well accepted and they gave me a big ovation after I finished.

"I took a taxi to meet my scheduled train back to Maine and arrived in Bangor, where my wife and children met me. It seemed good to be home to the wide-open spaces. I vowed that I would never want to go out of state again. But I want to tell you one thing, Doc, if you ever go down to that city of Boston—if they offer you clam chowder, you just better take it cause one way or the other, they're gonna get it into ya somehow." And he chuckled and chuckled.

14

Just Another Monday

It was three A.M. on Sunday morning, and I had just returned from seven hours of farm calls after a busy Saturday in the small-animal hospital. My rubber farm boots and coveralls off, I was tiptoeing through the kitchen trying not to disturb my family when the phone rang.

"That you, Doc?"

I recognized the reedy voice of Lucas, the adult son of one of my long-standing clients, Jim Thomas. "Yes, Lucas," I said, "it's me." Having spoken to him many times on the phone, I beat him to his next line. "How are things out your way?"

He stammered and stuttered. "Uh, ah, can you come right out here, uh, Doc?"

"What's the matter, Lucas?"

"I can't say nothin' over this party line," he muttered. "Mildred Farnham, down the road, she don't sleep too well, if you know what I mean."

"Lucas, it's late. Give me a hint."

"Look, Doc, trust me. We need you to come out as quick as you can, but go to the house first, 'cause Daddy wants to see ya before ya go to the barn."

"All right," I sighed. I did trust Lucas. Though he wasn't the sharpest knife in the drawer, he was an honest sort, and I knew something serious was afoot.

I pulled on my coveralls and rubber boots again and downed a slug of orange juice as I passed the refrigerator. It was April in mid-coast Maine, which is not the same thing as spring. Although there was no snow on the ground, the air had a sting to it as I slid into my car. The engine was still warm from the drive home from my last call.

Jim Thomas, Lucas's father, was typical of Maine dairy farmers in the early 1950s. His farm sprawled over about a hundred acres, of which about fifty were cleared and tillable. Jim's great-great-grandfather had carved the first ten acres out of the mixed pine and hardwood forest and built a humble but steadfast house with a rambling, shed-like ell attached to a cow barn. Jim and his family now occupied this compound, which had seen few improvements over the decades.

As I topped the hill overlooking Jim's place, a nearly full moon lit up every detail in the little valley below. The tableau conjured up my own upbringing on a farm in Vassalboro, about forty miles inland from my practice in Belfast. Even the higgledy-piggledy nest of structures was similar. My parents and Jim's parents, and the grandparents alike, had also struggled against the forces of nature to eke out a living off the land. I had seen barns burn, watched horses and cows die of disease or get killed in accidents. My siblings and I had gone without a lot of extras during the Great Depression, and we had worked as farmhands from the age of six. As a kid, I knew firsthand farming's risks and heartbreaks. As an adult, my work took me to similar painful episodes in the lives of other farmers.

I had become so preoccupied with my thoughts that I nearly missed Jim's driveway. Turning in at the last moment, I parked near the ell and entered the shed door. In the semi-dark (a dim, single lightbulb hung in the rear of the shed) I had to cross about fifteen feet to the kitchen door on a pair of century-old planks that bridged a cellar pit that the family used to store firewood. I was doing okay until I tripped on a spike about halfway across. That old nail had caught me before, but this time—probably because I was half blind with fatigue—it sent me tumbling into the woodpile four feet below. I landed with a clatter, tangled in stove wood, and my medical grip, the proverbial black bag, flew from my hand and scattered its contents all over the woodpile.

The fracas awoke Jim's son Lucas, who had been dozing at the kitchen table, and he appeared in the shed doorway. Next to him stood Rover, a shepherd-mutt with a mile-wide vicious streak. Jim always kept nasty dogs, leading me to suspect that, like many Depression-era farmers, he kept his cash under the mattress. But that was not at the top of my list of concerns at the moment.

"That you, Doc?" Lucas hollered, pointing the beam of a flashlight into the shed's dusty gloom.

"Down here!" I shouted. Rover snarled, exposing his impressive incisors.

"Jeekers," Lucas said. "What're you doin' down there?"

"Never mind," I said, collecting my loose gear as I talked. "Listen, why don't you leave that flashlight here and hitch up Rover near the barn. By the time you come back, I'll have this stuff gathered up."

"Ayuh," he said, tossing me the light. Clutching Rover's collar, he half-dragged the growling dog out the door.

When he returned a few minutes later, I had made my way out of the woodpile and back up into the shed, the contents of my medical bag secure. "We'd better go into the house, Doc. Daddy wants to talk to ya," Lucas said, shifting his feet. Something was up.

I followed Lucas through the farm's kitchen where I had sat on occasion, writing out treatment instructions and sipping instant coffee. But Jim was nowhere to be seen. Lucas silently continued through the old-fashioned front parlor, still furnished with the original Victorian horsehair sofa, and on to a rear bedroom. There on the bed lay Jim in a sweat-stained union suit, the sheets damp and bunched around him. He was conscious but gasping for breath, as if his next intake of air would be the last.

"That you, Braddie?" he croaked.

"Yes," I said.

"Got yer earphones with ya?" he rasped.

"Yeah, right here," I said, holding up the stethoscope that always dangled from my neck. I plugged the earpieces into my ears and bent over to place the cold bell on his chest. The instrument revealed the classic rales of pneumonia, some of the worst I'd ever heard.

"How long have you been sick?" I asked.

"'Bout three days," he gasped.

"You need a people doctor, Jim," I said.

Lucas interjected, "You know how Daddy feels about them, Doc. He thought you might have some medicine that would fix him up, seeing's how you told us most of the medicine's the same for people and animals."

I regretted dispensing that piece of information.

"Besides," Lucas continued, "we knew you'd come sooner and it wouldn't cost much on account of we got those sick cows." He stared down at the floor after this unaccustomed rush of words and shifted his feet some more.

I walked back out to the kitchen and phoned a physician friend of mine, who promptly ordered an ambulance. I went back to the bedroom and told Jim he was about to be carried off to the nearest hospital. He seemed disappointed, but he was far too weak to protest.

"After you look at them sick cows in the barn," he croaked, "Damon Scofield wants you to stop by and check his horse. It's ailin'."

I nodded, patted Jim's sweaty shoulder, and turned to follow Lucas out to the barn. "Hey, Doc," Jim called after me, "ya suppose they'll be taking any pictures of my lungs?"

"I imagine so," I replied.

"Well, I ain't payin' for no foolish pictures," he said. " I heard they don't mean a damned thing."

I just waved and turned again, but once more he called us back in a barely audible voice. "Doc, while you're out here, have a look at that gall on Dick." Dick was one of two draft horses on the farm. I agreed to look at Dick's elbow lesion.

While we picked our way carefully through the dark shed, Lucas said to me, "Guess you figured out that the main reason we called you was 'cause of Daddy, but we really do have these two cows that ain't breeding right."

We crossed to the barn past Rover, who reared up, gnashing his fangs and barking as we walked by. Lucas pointed out the cows in question, both young Guernseys. "They've been bred three or four times, but nothin' seems to stick," he said. "We thought you better take a look inside there."

I conducted a brief vaginal exam of each cow, and it was a good thing I did. The first had endometritis, which means that the entire uterus was infected, creating a painful inflammation. Human females can get the same condition. Lucas held up the cow's tail as I worked. First I injected the female hormon, estrogen, to induce the cervix to open. Then I carefully inserted antibiotic boluses— pills as big as shotgun shells that would attack the infection from inside. I would need to return in two or three days to repack the uterus. I left sulfanilamide tablets to be given by mouth.

Lucas then led me down to the next cow. "Funny thing 'bout

this one, Doc. I coulda swore she was pregnant. But after awhile she never got any bigger, then she missed her due date by more 'n a month. Now and then she kinda strains, like she's about to calve, but nothing comes out. She's off her feed for a day now."

An exam quickly revealed a condition called "mummified fetus" that often afflicts Guernsey cattle. At some point between the third and eighth month of pregnancy (like humans, cows carry fetuses for nine months), a genetic anomaly causes the fetus to die, and the fetus fails to fully decompose. In some cases the cow is able to expel it, but sometimes the fetus becomes dried out, causing it to get stuck. As the fetus deteriorates, bacteria can cause a life-threatening infection in the uterus.

I gave the cow a shot of estrogen to dilate the cervix. Over the next few days it might dilate enough to allow the cow to eject the fetus on her own. I told Lucas to call me if that didn't happen in three days, and I'd extract it by hand. She'd also need a shot of antibiotics. I would have to return in three days anyway to repack that other cow's infected uterus.

Lucas stared at me as if I were relating a tale about aliens. "Mummified? Jeekers," he muttered. But he agreed to call me either way.

Then we moved to where Dick, the draft horse, was tethered. I examined his sore elbow, which at this point was a bare spot where the floor had gradually worn the hair away when Dick was lying down or rising. I applied a tincture of iodine to the sore and left a four-ounce bottle of gentian violet.

"Better give old Dick some time off until that heals," I told Lucas. "Put this on once a day until he gets a nice scab going. When the scab falls off, you can work him again." I also told him to make a sheepskin padding to cover the horse's elbow.

It was almost four-thirty A.M. when I finished up, and Lucas headed out to start the milking. I slid into my car and drove the three miles to the Scofield place. I startled Damon in the milk-room, where he was just putting the milking machines together.

"Doc!" he said amiably. "Jim musta told you I wanted to see you."

I asked what the problem was.

"Well, you know that damned foolish horse of mine—that drafter?" he said. "She's got some kinda skin humor."

"How long's she had it?" I asked.

"Cripes, I don't know. But it's gotten real bad the last two or three months."

I sighed. "Which way is she?"

He scratched his armpit absently. "I think she's outdoors some-where. Let's take a little grain in a bucket and maybe we can find her." Damon trotted to the house to ask his wife to start the milk-ing and returned with two flashlights and a bucket of grain.

"Does she do a lot of scratching, Damon?" I asked, throwing a few things into my medical bag; it served as a portable field surgi-cal kit.

"I guess to hell she does," he snorted. "This horse tears up fences, rubbing up against every fence post I got. Tore some of 'em clean out. Cows've been getting out." He paused. "Y'know, a horse dealer stopped by and I asked him to take a look at it. He told me to bathe her in Fels Naphtha soap, that lye stuff. So I did."

"Yeah, I know the stuff," I said. My family had made lye soap on our farm when I was growing up. "What happened after you bathed her?"

"Well, that horse was some contrary about gettin' a bath," he said. "Had a hell of a time with her at first, but after doing it about twice a week the last two weeks, damned if she didn't come out and just rattle that old washtub when it come time for the next bath. But I could see it weren't helping her." He sighed. "It was one of them exercises in fertility."

Smiling, I started to ask another question, but Damon cut me off. "Then I asked the postman to have a look at her," he continued. "He allowed that horses need to eat a mixture of ground-up vegetables, mostly turnip and potato tubers. So I fed 'er that mash for about a week, but I couldn't see it helped a mite."

"Well," I said, as we stumbled through the hummocky pasture in the gray, predawn light. "I hope we find her soon, I have a big day ahead of me."

But Damon wasn't through with his tale. "You know that guy, Horry, who trades horses at the state fairs?"

"Yeah," I sighed. Horry was the town drunk in three different towns.

"He was passing through, so I says, 'Why don't you take a peek at that skin humor on my horse?' Horry, he was half in the bag, but he told me to rub some cylinder oil on it."

"New or used?" I quipped. Damon didn't get the joke.

"Just said oil," he shrugged. "I plastered on some old used crankcase oil out of the tractor, but that ain't made one speck of difference either."

By now I knew the narrative would keep going. "Then what did you do?" I asked.

He looked surprised. "I asked around when you might be comin' out this way," he said, stating what was clearly obvious to him. "Couldn't afford to pay your travelin' fee," he added sheepishly.

Just then we heard steps and Damon's wife, Angie, caught up with us.

"Hi, Doc," she said. "I just wanted to ask if the humor could have anything to do with the sugar I've been feeding her. I give her about a cup a day. It's her big treat."

"I doubt it, Angie," I said. She looked relieved and headed back to the barn.

Damon and I stomped through a patch of juniper bordering the woods. "She likes hanging around down here next to the brook," he said with a chuckle. I wasn't seeing much humor in our expedition, but I said nothing. We probed the fringe of the woods along the brook, circled back through the neighbor's pasture, and returned to the barn. It was now daylight and heavy dew sparkled on the meadow. "Well, Damon...," I began.

Then we both spotted the horse standing in the doorway of a hovel attached to the cow barn—her usual domicile. "Hang blame it, Doc!" Damon shouted. "I should have known she'd come back here."

"Yeah," I said. My bones ached with weariness. "Let's get on with it."

Damon held the horse's halter, and I examined the inflamed skin along her flanks. The "skin humor" proved to be fungal dermatitis, commonly known as ringworm. My nose caught a familiar odor. "Why did you use kerosene with the cylinder oil, Damon?"

"Oh, guess I forgot to mention that, Doc," he said. "My other neighbor says kerosene is good for any kind of skin humor. I had some, so I just mixed it in with the cylinder oil."

"Well," I said, "I'm afraid you have just made things worse, like rubbing salt into the wound." The skin was now raw, no doubt far more inflamed than when the treatment began.

Damon looked crestfallen. I was in no mood to cheer him up, so I silently proceeded to give the poor beast a large intramuscular injection of vitamin A, which helps maintain the integrity of the skin, allowing it to fight fungus. When I was done I told Damon to get into town and buy a quart of cod liver oil, which contains a variety of vitamins, especially A and D, and a bottle of Head and Shoulders shampoo. "Shampoo the bad spots twice a week," I instructed, "then wipe it, rinse it, and when the skin dries, rub in the cod liver oil as hard as you can. Wear rubber gloves"

He looked baffled now. "Huh. I thought cod liver oil could only help if you took it by mouth," he said.

"That's true to an extent," I said, "but we just gave her a big dose of vitamin A, one of the active ingredients in cod liver oil, so she's going to get that working inside her body, too. Both will make her skin healthy again. This is a fungus, and fungus doesn't like healthy skin. And the dandruff shampoo will kill off the fungus while the skin heals." I also told him to put the horse outside on sunny days to absorb more vitamins A and D from the sun.

"Makes sense, I guess," he nodded. "Why the gloves?"

"It's like athlete's foot—you could get it just as easily as the horse did."

"Roger that, Doc," he said.

I walked back to the barn, drained a little of the disinfectant from my pail onto my rubber farm boots, and scrubbed them down as I always did, to prevent spreading diseases from one farm to another. I packed up my kit and pail and once more slid behind the wheel, picturing hot coffee and one of the donuts from the store at the four corners down the road.

I heard a tap at my window. I rolled it down as Angie leaned in. "Doc, I almost forgot. While you're here, could you please take a look at a calf we got out back? It's awful scrawny and not growing well."

I got out and followed her into the barn, walking way to the back where loose hay was strewn and about ten little calves were tethered. I spotted the sick one instantly; it was as thin as a razor. After a quick examination, I found that all the animal's lymph glands were enlarged.

"I'm sorry, but I think the calf has lymphogenous leukemia," I told Angie. By now Damon had joined us. I took out a syringe and drew some blood to send to a lab to confirm the diagnosis, because a number of general infections could also cause the glands to swell.

I gave them a brief description of this form of blood cancer.

"Cancer?" Damon said. "I just thought she was sick."

"Is it catching, Doc?" Angie asked.

"No. We can wait until I get the test results back," I said. Once more I washed up, stowed my gear in the car, and backed out of the driveway knowing that I was almost certainly looking at a terminal case.

This time I made it all the way out of the driveway and drove straight to the general store, where coffee and a plain donut had to provide sustenance in lieu of a night's sleep. And, I must say, they tasted pretty good.

I'm happy to say Jim was back home after five or six days in the hospital, the two cows came along fine and had future offspring, Damon had to shoot the calf with cancer, but his workhorse regained a healthy hide.

15

Know-It-All Lonnie Boy

I got home around three A.M. from barn rounds one winter morning, and on the telephone pad was a note to call Lonnie Boy. My wife knew Lonnie Boy as well as I did. He ran a large dairy farm down in Lincoln County. I called Lonnie and got him on the phone.

He allowed that he had been trying to deliver a calf from a first-calf heifer. He went on and on bragging about his prowess and talent for delivering calves for anyone within twenty miles of him, but he now had one he couldn't quite deal with. He said he had the neighbors in, lots of help, and they had been at it for a couple of days.

"What do you need me for, Lonnie?" I asked.

He said, "Well, I've got to get that calf out of the cow. The calf is dead anyway—I know that because I pulled the head off with a come-along. I gave up then and called Ed McDonald; he's a pretty good vet, you know. He spent a couple hours but he gave up. So I said to myself, there's only one vet that I know that can get that calf out, and that's Dr. Brown up to Belfast. So anyway, I'd appreciate it if you'd come down. I'm going to be sleeping in my chair in the living room right next to the window, so when you drive in to the milkroom dooryard, just walk across the yard and tap on the window. I'll come out and help you. I need a couple more hours sleep if I can get it. I'm exhausted. Been up two days trying to get that calf out."

Probably about forty minutes later I pulled into his driveway and parked my car in front of his milkroom. I looked across the yard, through the window and saw Lonnie Boy asleep in his overstuffed chair. I said to myself, "I may as well look at the patient first." So I walked into the cow barn and down the ramp to where the cows were. I saw this poor pathetic heifer, all bedraggled, with a big calf protruding from her vagina. There was no head on the calf. The head was on the floor, off to the side.

My first thought was to get the heifer out of pain. I gave her a pint of 50 percent dextrose to give her energy, and then gave her a spinal epidural. This would also stop her straining and allow me to work on her internally. I would need a lot of freedom to get that calf out.

I went to the milkroom and got a pail to mix up an iodine solution as a disinfectant. While I was doing that I noticed a supersized box of Ivory dish detergent. "There!" I said, grabbing it.

Then I stripped to the waist to save my clothes. I lay down in the gutter behind the heifer and slowly but surely and very methodically started to lubricate the obstructed areas between the mother and the baby with the Ivory soap. There was a complete hip lock. The highest point of the hips on the calf had locked into the shaft of the mother's ileum. After about a half-hour of lubricating and re-lubricating the involved areas and then gathering all the strength I had plus a little more, I was able to rotate that little calf's pelvis so that it finally freed itself from its mother's pelvis. I proceeded then to lubricate the rest of the body and was able to slip the rest of the calf out very easily. I had thought I would have to dismember the calf to get it out of the mother, but I was able to get it out with dish soap.

Just One More Thing, Doc

After I washed up, I went into the icy yard and walked over to the window, where Lonnie was asleep on the other side. I tapped on the window lightly and he started out of the chair like a cobra. He quickly saw me and said, "I'll be right out."

I hurried back across the icy yard and into the barn, since I didn't want to miss the expression on his face when he saw that the job was done.

He came in through the barn door and started to walk down by the cows to where the patient was. He gave the head a little kick and looked at the rest of the calf. Finally coming to he said, "How in hell did you ever get that calf out of that heifer?"

I said, "Actually, Lonnie, it was one of the easier deliveries I've had. If it hadn't been for a box of Ivory dish soap, Lonnie, and a lot of strategic maneuvering inside her, it would have been pretty complicated. But I think anyone could have figured it out."

At this point he was getting a little embarrassed and I had deflated his ego substantially. But he recovered enough to say, "While you're here, Doc, I've got a mess of heifers out back, four, five months old, that have a lot of extra teats on 'em. Will you go take care of it for me?"

I got my automatic syringe and loaded it with procaine, a local anesthetic, and got my large surgical scissors. I quickly dispensed with that work.

As I was getting ready to leave, Lonnie said, "While you're here, Doc, I'd like you to get a look at my new car." We walked across the yard, then across the road to a two-car garage. There sat a brand new Buick automobile. But both sides were badly wrecked. It had been in some kind of crash.

I said, "You didn't buy that car that way did you, Lonnie?"

And he said, "No. I'll tell you the story. My brother and I went down to the Buick garage and we both bought identical cars with identical options."

"Is his all smashed up too?" I interrupted.

"Yup. I'll tell you how this all happened. Larry and I have always been competitive. When we got bicycles as kids we used to race 'em up and down this road. We'd bet allowances. I would bet my allowance against his that I could beat him from that tree you see down there next to the garage to there. So it got to be a habit, and the same thing happened when we got automobiles. He was always trying to outrace me.

"So anyway, my brother said, 'How about if we race these cars for $100? Winner take all.' I asked him, 'Where you want to do it?' He said, 'Where we always do—on the lake. The ice is still good.'

"So we took the cars and got them down to the lake. We started and he would get ahead of me a little and then I would get ahead of him a little. The end of the lake was coming up and we knew we were probably going to crash, so we both started to slide sideways. We thought we could stop, but brakes didn't work on the ice. Larry's Buick hit some rocks that were sticking up out of the ice near the shore. It brought him up short in front of me and I hit him. What a hell of a collision! That's how I wrecked my right side into his left side."

I had to break in, "But both sides are wrecked; how'd that happen?"

"You won't believe it. We flipped to see who would get the tractor to pull the car off of the rocks. I lost, so I went up to get the Case tractor with the chains on it. We pulled his car back onto the ice and we set about racing back the length of the lake—the first one down there would win the $100.

"So off we went, and it was kind of a repeat of the first race up. We got up pretty good speed and he would nose ahead and relax; then I would go faster and nose by him and settle out. This time I got near the end of the lake first and ended up on the rocks—and Larry couldn't stop. I got hit on the other side. So did he.

"He keeps saying his insurance company is going to take care of my car. I keep telling him that mine will take care of his. I sure hope so, 'cause I want my front fenders painted with fire flames."

As we walked back to my car, Lonnie kept shaking his head, saying he still couldn't see how I got that calf out of that cow.

"Well," I said, "You thought you could get it out using brute force and ignorance. I like to think I did it smarter. I hope you learn something out of this, Lonnie."

He said, "Well, I'll give it to you, Doc. You're a damn good vet."

"Thank you, Lonnie." I was a little surprised, because he was such a braggart and know-it-all.

That next summer I was at a fair when who did I run into? Lonnie Boy, of course. I passed him and we bid each other a hello. I couldn't resist asking, "How's your calving going? Had any tough ones lately?"

He turned and looked the other way. Not much to say, I guess. Possibly because he was with his buddy, another dairy farmer, and didn't want to discuss the subject of calving cases, especially the one last winter.

16

All the Way Across

The phone rang at five o'clock in the morning. A farmer from Searsmont, Maine, was calling to say that one of his cows had her teat ripped off and it was hanging by a thread and bleeding badly. Her stablemate had stepped on it during the night. Of course he wanted me to come as quickly as I could. My wife shook me awake in my overstuffed chair.

I took a little orange juice for energy, jumped in my car, and drove to Jim's place. When I got there I found that he had described the situation perfectly. The teat was just hanging by the skin. I anesthetized the area with procaine. About half an hour later I had placed innumerable stitches in the teat and it looked normal once again.

I had completed the procedure and was picking up so I could be on my way when Jim said, "While you're here, Doc, I wondered if you could look at my new coon dog that I got from Virginia the other day. He's got an eye problem. It keeps running all the time." He went in the house and then came out with an adorable coon dog pup, which was about three months old. Sure enough, he had a condition called entropion. The lower eyelid was rolled in and resting on the cornea, the transparent part of the eye.

He brought the dog in to my office the following Tuesday, and

I performed a simple operation to reposition the rolled part of the lower eyelid so that it never bothered him again. There is a similar condition, usually seen in larger dogs, called ectopion, where the eyelid rolls outward; it is as easily treated as entropion. Both genetic anomalies will produce a lifetime of eye infections if not corrected. Jim's puppy made great progress and became a great coon hound. Jim just adored him.

When I left Jim's that day after treating his cow, I took a short-cut to Nash's Store in Freedom. It involved crossing a tiny little bridge made of planks that were two by tens, about twelve feet long. The stream was small, and I had crossed the bridge many times over the years without incident. Not this time, however.

I made it to the middle of the bridge and suddenly the front end of the car fell through the planks as they snapped and broke. I got out and found the rear bumper of my '59 Chevrolet resting on the dirt road behind me, at the south end of the bridge.

Looking around, I spotted a torn-down chicken house nearby and pilfered several strong planks. I jacked up the car, positioned the planks, and drove over the temporarily repaired bridge.

About ten minutes later I arrived at Norm Nash's Country Store, where I usually stopped to pick up something to eat when I was on the go in that area. I had told Norm I would give his four Walker coon hounds rabies vaccinations the next time I was by. He, like so many others, would call my office and say he had something that needed doing but he could wait until I was out his way conveniently. I kept these jobs-to-do in a book entitled "When you're out my way, Doc."

While we were doing the vaccinations I told him about the tiny bridge incident, since Norm was the first selectman of the town at the time.

He said, "No wonder. Alton Peavey and his overloaded pulp truck were just through here, and Alton reported that the bridge cracked when he went over it. So it wasn't your fault, Doc. In fact, at the town meeting last week we raised a thousand dollars to replace that little bridge. We're going to use steel from now on."

Norm paused for a moment with a chuckle, and then went on. "George Mellon stood up at the meeting and said he wanted us to shorten the bridge—it didn't need to be as long as it was. He said he had measured the width of that little brook and could urinate halfway across it. Ben Chambers, our moderator, said 'You are out of order, George.' George shot back, 'I know I'm out of order, otherwise I could urinate all the way across it.'"

I left the store laughing and proceeded to head towards Montville, where I had another farm call along with a when-you're-by call. Then it was back to my small-animal hospital for surgeries and appointments.

17

A Few Evening Barn Rounds

T ime was always of the essence. Over the years I learned every shortcut in every town in five counties. But there were never enough hours in the day.

On this particular evening I was going to the Lufkin farm in Brooks. Ben was still up. We did many pregnancy checks and a couple of nonbreeder sterility jobs. In doing rectal pregnancy checks on cows and horses, the hazards include getting kicked in the chest, stomach, or anywhere on the front of the body. I was sometimes hobbled for days because of a hard kick, but most of those injuries didn't result in broken bones.

I recall one mare that I was going to give a pregnancy check. She was very fractious so I gave her a sedative—I anticipated some trouble. I succeeded in getting my arm into the rectum and was making my determination when she suddenly reared up on me and came over backwards. Somehow I was able to retrieve my arm in a split second, but she managed to knock me down and ended up on her side on top of me. She struggled to her four feet and I got up on my two. It was nothing short of a miracle that I still have two healthy arms today. I do, however, have a lot of indentations in my shins.

Next I was off to the Brown farm. It was a half-hour away. I had been warned by the call from the office that Ralph had gotten a new dog from a junkyard somewhere to guard the property. I was supposed to avoid the milkroom in the front of the barn because Ruffy protected that whole area at night and would attack me. I was instructed to walk around the barn and go through the back door to the tie-up, and then go down the length of the barn to the milkroom, where I'd find the list of things to do.

However, I didn't do that when I arrived. I went to the back of my car, opened the trunk, loaded a pail with what I thought I'd need, and grabbed my long-handled boot brush that I used to wash my footwear between farm visits. I had the brush in my right hand along with my flashlight and the pail in my left hand. I could see Ruffy at a respectable distance, tugging at his chain and showing his forty-four teeth. He definitely wanted to attack me.

I was undeterred and started walking toward the milkroom about twenty feet away, with Ruffy threatening me every step. Then all of a sudden, when I had reached the milkroom door, he kind of settled down, turned, and dragged his chain back to the doghouse. We eventually became pretty good pals. Ralph told me that I was the only person he ever knew who was able to come in that milkroom door, unattended, without Ruffy tearing them to pieces.

I found Ralph's list on the bulk tank in the mil room. There were cows to check for pregnancy. And as usual, there was a "while-you're-here, Doc" note that wanted me to check number eight's right hind leg. It was lame and made it hard for her to get up. Usually in such a case I gave a shot of depomedral, which is a long-acting steroid, into the joint.

I wrote Ralph a note on the calendar, recording every cow that I had checked for pregnancy and the one that I had injected. I packed up and proceeded to the next town.

Knox was about seven miles away, and I arrived at the Larrabee farm ten minutes later. They were still up. Lee Larrabee, the owner, along with his only son, Jack, had a big herd of cows. Lee had started the farm with seven acres and a dump truck. He used the dump truck to haul loads of gravel for the state. Every time he could free up some money, he would buy a cow. After he had ten cows he decided that he would work in the woods to make up any difference. And from that roughly ten cows came the farm with 600 head of cattle. They also owned about 1,600 acres of land to farm. They were milking 400 cows twice a day. It was quite an operation, as it still is today.

Jack was married and had two boys. Nobody ever worked harder than Jack Larrabee. His sons have the same work ethic and put away a pile of work. They never stand still and are always looking for something to improve their efficiency, from farm equipment to milking devices—anything to stay on top of it. They're a good example of success in dairy farming.

After I finished my work there, Velma Larrabee invited me in for coffee and doughnuts, which provided some quick energy. I had two more calls to make. One was a quick call next door (five miles), to Yeaton's farm to take the blood of one of Iddo Yeaton's cows. One cow had produced a test reaction to brucellosis, and it was time for the next test to see if she had cleared or was worse. The other visit was to the Price farm. Ron and Trudy Price operated their Craneland Farm from dawn till dark 365 days a year. They knew no end to work and were excellent caretakers of their registered herd of Holstein cows, some of the best around. They were equally prudent tillers of their land.

I went into the Prices' milkroom and on the bulk tank was the list of my work. It consisted mostly of cow pregnancy checks and a couple of hard breeders (cows having a difficult time getting pregnant). At three-thirty A.M. I was about ready to head for home when Ron walked into the barn for the A.M. milking. As with so many farmers, you could set your watch on his arrival to his barns at milking time. We reviewed what I had done on his list and I was off to Belfast.

I arrived back at the office at about four A.M. I checked all the animals that were hospitalized, including the surgery patients that I had done that day, and medicated two or three of them. Then I headed to my home in town a mile away. I went to the kitchen, to the big double stove where my devoted, lovely wife had left me a wonderful meal in the warming oven.

I took it into the front room on a tray, grabbed my billing materials, and worked on both my supper and the bills. Within fifteen minutes I had fallen asleep.

At six A.M. my wife came downstairs and shook me awake to tell me that the office phone had rung. The Bartlett farm had called with a cow that had a teat hanging by a thread—another case of the cow next to her stepping on her udder, tearing the teat. It was bleeding quite badly. I needed to get there as soon as possible.

I sat in the kitchen with my wife for a few minutes and discussed the children, what they were doing, and what was coming up. Then I went out the door and started my car, beginning another twenty- to twenty-two-hour day.

Just One More Thing, Doc

18

Two Milking Disasters

A farmer whose farm was located in Swanville, Maine, about seven miles from my office, called one day to say that when he started milking his cows, the first three had died. He wanted me to come out as quickly as I could. I told him not to milk any more cows until I got there.

I left my medical tasks at the hospital, as I often had to, and hurried to the farm. When I arrived I could see burn marks on the carcasses that looked typical of electrocution. Now to find out why.

Ed had inherited an old farm, but he didn't want to follow the old system of hand-milking cows that his father and grandfather had used in that barn for over a hundred years. He used an electric milking machine. When I was in the seventh and eighth grades one of my farm chores was to milk nine cows, by hand, before and after school. This took about two hours. Once our farm was electrified in 1938 it took an hour or less to milk our entire herd with the new milking machine. This meant I could sleep an extra hour in the morning. The milking calluses on my hands disappeared within about a month.

A milking machine needs to create a vacuum to draw the milk from the cow's udder. The four teat cups are attached to the udder, and the vacuum pump, controlled by a pulsator, sucks milk out of two quarters of the udder, releases, and allows the vacuum to be transferred to the other two quarters of the udder. It keeps alternating until the cow is completely milked.

Ed's cows wore metal neck chains, and in his milking machine setup he preferred to hook them up while he milked them.

In spite of being set on rubber washers, the electric motor running Ed's milking machine vibrated almost violently when it started up, causing the small electrical supply wires to chafe. This was made worse by Ed's habit of turning the motor off between cows to save on electricity. Over time the insulation covering had rubbed off, baring the wires. This made the device an electric chair, especially for metallically restrained, cloven-hoofed animals. Electricity dances along a pipe or anything metal trying to get to ground, and what better way than through a cow, killing her in the process.

Going over Ed's milking system I found where the wires had chafed and told him, as I had advised many farmers before, to install a foot-long piece of rubber radiator hose into the vacuum line to prevent electricity from going into the line and presenting a danger to the cows.

I was always intimidated by electrical storms and accidental electrocutions. It was due to an incident when I was eighteen years old. I was working on my grandfather's farm that summer, and one Saturday I'd been entrusted by my elders to do the evening milking while they took a little time off to go to a church supper about thirty miles away. At four P.M. sharp I got the cows into the barn from the pasture and got the milking machines ready, along with hot water for cleaning the udders before milking.

As I tied up the last cow I heard thunder off in the distance. Having been through many electrical storms at the farm, I judged it was too far away to be any danger to the task at hand, so I went about my milking. In about an hour and a half I had finished milking the fifteen cows. I placed all the milk in the little milkroom attached to the barn, where it would be separated into cream and skim milk. The cream from our cows was sold mainly for ice cream, and the skim milk was fed to the calves, pigs, and chickens.

Suddenly there was an ear-shattering clap and the next thing I was aware of, I was lying on the wet floor of the milkroom. The first thing I saw was black smoke spewing in from the door that led out to the tie-up, where the cows were. I checked my arms and legs, which seemed to be present and unhurt, then I jumped to my feet and went as fast as I could back into the tie-up to release the cows. Nine were still on their feet, and I shooed them outdoors as quickly as they would go. I got a garden hose, hooked it up in the barn, and put out the fire that had started on the wall near the tie-up.

Then it was time to check the six cows that didn't walk out of the barn. I raced to the phone in the farmhouse and called the vet in Waterville, who arrived in twenty minutes. It was obvious that they were dead, and he wrote a death certificate stating that electricity had killed them. We'd need this later for the insurance company.

Lightning had struck a tree near the north end of the barn. Attached to that tree was an electric fence. The bolt of lightning came through the fence to the steel tie chains in the barn. The fuse box exploded through the wall out into the barnyard about fifty feet. The charge continued on into the wiring in the milkroom, where it struck the water cooler and everything electrical in there.

The surviving cows had been hooked up to a wooden rafter in the barn. The cows that died had been hooked up to metal stan-chions. I had been stupidly sitting on the cooler in the milkroom, which is why I got thrown to the floor by the bolt and knocked unconscious.

The only thing I can say is that I lived to tell the story; six cows didn't. The barn was damaged but I prevented a complete loss by getting the hose on the fire quickly.

When my grandparents returned from the church supper, we all went to the barn. I explained what happened as well as I could, and my grandfather said he was very glad that I was alive and that he was proud of what I had done. He said that now I was a man, that I had done what a mature adult would have done in a tough situation. For my grandfather to give anyone praise was unusual, so I was very proud.

The insurance company paid for the six dead cows and paid for new electrical motors for the vacuum line, the milk separator, and the milk cooler. We were also able to have an electrician rewire the barn. We got rid of the metal neck chains—they were the final reason for the electrocution of the six cows.

19

Inside Out

Over the years I replaced many everted uteri in cows. This is also known as prolapse of the uterus, or what farmers call cast withers. In horses it is not so common—in fact it's an unusual event.

A lady who raised Arabian horses on the outskirts of Belfast called my office and and said that her favorite Arabian mare, Smartie, had foaled and the foaling bed and bladder had come out of her vagina. The mare had stood up in the stall instinctively to suckle the foal and was awfully upset. To make things worse, Smartie was banging the uterus and bladder against the stall walls. The organs were bleeding profusely.

In fifteen minutes I was there. One look at the mare's sclera (the white supporting tissue of the eye) told me she had lost too much blood. I gave her an injection of coagamine and vitamin K, which help in clotting blood. Then I took three quarts of blood from Charley, an old draft horse the owner kept around to cultivate her big vegetable garden in the summer. I gave the blood to Smartie and also gave her a spinal to stop her straining. She lay down then and stopped straining, which made it much easier for me to replace the uterus and bladder.

I started by washing the uterus and bladder with a mild solution of tamed iodine. With an antiseptic soap powder that would cleanse and lubricate the skin, I disinfected my own hands and the owner's, as she would be helping me replace the organs. About a half-hour later the uterus and bladder were back in Smartie where they belonged.

Smartie then got an injection of posterior pituitary hormone to contract the smooth muscle of the uterus and to prevent further straining. I packed the inside of the uterus with antibiotic boluses, and she also got a dose of bi-cillin, a long-acting form of penicillin.

I'm happy to report that Smartie made a complete recovery. She came into estrus in cycle and produced another normal foal by normal delivery by herself a year later. She went on to have several more foals over the years. Every time I was at the farm to treat other horses, Smartie would whinny and snicker and act restless until I went over to her and stroked her face and mane with my hand. She was always very kind and gentle and seemed to be thanking me for taking care of her when things were bad.

20

A Defective Pill Gun

Doris called and said that Missy—her true love, her pride and joy, her horse—was acutely lame. She wanted me to stop by when I could over the next couple of days.

Doris lived with Harvey, who was a small dairy farmer in a small town. He had a few cows, and on the side he was a cattle and machinery auctioneer. Harvey was a real character. He stuttered terribly and reminded me of Mel Tillis, the great country/western singer. Put a guitar in Mel Tillis's hands and he didn't stutter. The same was true with Harvey: put an auctioneer's gavel in his hands and he stopped stuttering. But in a normal conversation he would say repeatedly, "Is that right? Is-is-is-is that right?" Then he would follow it up with, "Re-re-re-really? Really?"

I went down on the second day from her call and found that Missy the horse had navicular disease. The tendon that attaches to the tiny bone at the end the hoof is called the navicular bone. It gets its name because the bone is boat-shaped. The tendon that passes under it can become irritated and can cause tendonitis, a lot of pain, and can eventually lead to osteitis, an inflammation of the bone itself.

I wrote out instructions for her blacksmith so that some corrections could be made the next time she was shod. In addition to that, I gave Missy an injection of Butazolidin, an anti-inflammatory drug used by man and beast. I left a box of Butazolidin tablets to be given with the balling gun, the device that a farmer uses to give pills to a large animal.

I asked Harvey if he had one and he said yes, it was still in pretty good shape. I told him what Missy needed and when he should give her the pills.

A couple of days later they called me up and reported that the end of the balling gun was missing. Doris said that she thought that Harvey had lost it intentionally 'cause he never really liked Missy. I said that I didn't think that was the case and that I'd be down to take a look.

She said that Missy was swallowing repeatedly, drooling constantly, and retching with her neck stretched. When I got there I found that the balling gun barrel was missing and that Doris was right about the horse's condition. I examined the esophagus from the outside and found that it was constantly swallowing. There was only one thing to do.

I got out my stomach tube and lubricated it with mineral oil. I passed it through Missy's nostril and down into the esophagus. I kept probing and probing gently until I touched on a hard object. I kept nudging it until I felt it slip into the stomach. At first I thought that that was that. Then my second thought was, could she pass the object in her manure? So I took two quarts of mineral oil and my stomach pump and pumped the oil into her stomach. Then I told Doris to call me in two days if the object didn't pass.

The very next day she called to report success. All was well. A couple of weeks later I had to drop by there to tend a sick cow and as I pulled into their driveway, I saw Doris riding Missy on her daily trail out through the pasture. Missy wasn't limping. Doris said the horse was back to her regular routine.

Just One More Thing, Doc

Before I left that day Doris asked me to show Harvey how to use their new balling gun. I lubricated a pill with mineral oil, put it in the balling gun, and gave the pill to Missy. But I surprised them both with the second pill. I put some mineral oil on it, put it in my hand, opened Missy's mouth, pulled her tongue out to the right side, went in with my left hand over the molars and teeth, put the tablet in the back of her throat, and she swallowed it. Harvey didn't know what to think.

I turned to him and said, "Harvey, don't ever try it that way."

And he said, with his stutter, "D-d-d-don't ever worry. I'm not that b-b-brave. But I just happened to think, while yer here, D-d-doc, I've got five or six calves that need to be vaccinated against bru-bru-bru-cellosis."

So I went about it. Just as I was getting ready to leave, Harvey said, "Just one more thing, Doc. I want you to pinch a bull. He's about five months old. We want to eat him in a couple of years, so we want him castrated."

So I got my emasculatome and we went in and did that. The emasculatome is an instrument for what they call a closed or non-surgical castration. Ideally it is done when the bull calf is between four and six months old. After about ten months it is not as effective and you should probably resort to a surgical castration. The secret with the emasculatome is to locate the vas deferens and pinch it, causing scar tissue and a blockage. Within several months the scrotum atrophies and shrivels up, and the testicles start to atrophy a little bit also. This is a sign of success, and the animal ends up a steer and not a bull. The inexperienced find it difficult to palpate the vas deferens amongst the other seven anatomical structures that make up the spermatic chord, or fail to pinch one side or the other; in either case you end up with a bull instead of a steer.

Just before I left, I said, "Now, Harvey, if you're going to give any tablets to a cow or a horse barehanded, for God's sake don't try it on a cow. If you try to do it barehanded on a cow like I did with Missy, you will probably lose a finger. They have a big, big hump at the back of their tongues, and I think it would cause you great problems."

He said, "You-you-you-you-you don't have t-t-t-to w-w-w-worry a-a-a-a-about th-th-th-that, re-re-re-re-really!"

Hardware Disease

As prey animals, cattle were designed by nature to quickly graze in the early hours of the morning, then hide in the woods where they'd regurgitate the food they had gulped down earlier and remasticate or "chew their cud." All ruminants have a hard dental pad instead of upper teeth in the front of the jaw. When they are grazing on pasture or eating hay in the winter, they'll unknowingly ingest nails, pieces of barbed wire, and other metal objects along with the grass or hay because this pad is so toughthey don't feel the foreign objects.

When they chew their cud, these foreign bodies stay down in the first compartment of the stomach, which is called the reticulum. But peristalsis, the muscular movement that brings the food up and down along the digestive tract, can cause things with sharp ends to poke through into the peritoneal cavity, causing fevers and infections and other ailments, even death. We call this problem collectively "hardware disease," and it's a common ailment in cattle.

It's similar to appendicitis in humans, when the appendix bursts and spills the contents into the body's abdominal cavity, causing severe peritonitis and septicemia (blood poisoning). In the old days this always meant death. The same is true in animals once they have peritonitis from hardware disease

During morning surgery one day, the front office let me know that Dr. Whitten from the University of Maine had called and wanted to speak with me. Dr. Whitten was a professor and chairman of the Veterinary Sciences Department of the university. I had taken two courses with him when I was an undergraduate student. One was general physiology and the other was bovine anatomy. He was very instrumental in getting students into vet school, including myself.

Dr. Whitten also oversaw the university's cattle herd, which was comprised of Ayrshires, Jerseys, Guernseys, and Holstein-Friesians. These were all purebred, registered cattle. The reason for his call was that one of his top-producing Holstein-Friesian cows was thought to have a displaced abomasum (fourth stomach), according to Dr. Whitten. He asked if I could come and give him a second opinion. Since the only treatment for such a condition is surgery, I prepared a surgery tray so that I could operate if necessary.

When I arrived in Orono, Dr. Whitten and I went directly to the barn. Dr. Whitten had been right; the cow had a severely displaced fourth stomach, so I prepared for surgery. About that time students started to gather, since I was going to do the operation in the old show ring, which had seating arrangements for about a hundred or so people. It soon filled up with students and faculty.

I set about to anesthetize the cow by giving her a spinal anesthetic, marking off lumbar nerves #1, 2, and 3 and filtrating the surgery site with local anesthesia. I couldn't resist holding the scalpel high over my head—and the crowd gasped deeply as I made a fourteen-inch incision down the cow's flank. I continued to open the abdomen, cutting through the muscles and the peritoneum, which lines the entire abdominal cavity. Then I put on a sterile sleeve and explored the situation. The abomasum was severely displaced, so we put her in dorsal recumbency—that is, up on her back. I managed to do what they call an abomasoplexy with the assistance of Dr. Whitten. I tacked the fourth stomach in a permanent location so that it wouldn't get displaced again. Then we sewed her up.

The anethetic wore off and the cow rose to her feet. We put her back in her stanchion and I gave her about a 1,000 c. of dextrose with some ACTH (adrenocorticotropic hormone) and instructed Dr. Whitten about her aftercare. Dr. Whitten asked if I had any interest in taking over as the university's vet for the herd. It would give him some relief since he was tired and getting older. I told him that I would fill in when possible.

When I made my first trip back to Orono to do some vet work on the herd, Dr. Whitten said that cow was doing wonderfully, had come back to full milk production, and was acting as if nothing had ever happened. I checked her for pregnancy that day and found her with calf. That made him even happier.

I was about ready to leave and head back to Belfast when the herdsman, Mr. Young, came up and asked, "Just one more thing, Doc. I got a cow that's really in bad shape; I should have called you a long time ago. She's arched up, she's sore, and her milk production has dropped to zero. She's off her feed and looks like a scarecrow. I got a temp of 103 from her."

I noticed one thing that stood out as I looked at her. She had a false jugular pulse, which is a pathognomonic symptom (a sign of one specific disease or ailment). My stethoscope was picking up a sound like a threshing machine near her heart. The systole, the left ventricle, was making a slapping noise and the mitral valve had an insufficiency. Listening from another perspective I could hear that the beat was muffled, indicating fluid between the pericardium and the heart. There were no S sounds in the heart. This was a weird one. I hadn't seen a heart problem this one in a cow like in a long, long time.

I decided that I should check her for hardware disease. Using my stethoscope I determined that she had something metallic in her tripe, the lining of the first stomach. I discussed this with Dr. Whitten and said, "We ought to do an exploratory on her and see what's going on in there." He agreed, so I prepared her for surgery.

I anesthetized her with a spinal block on lumbar nerves #1, 2, and 3 and filtrated the surgical site. I incised the right flank in much the same fashion as I used with the cow with the displaced abomasum, put on a sterile sleeve, and started to explore the abdomen. The reticulum was adhering to the diaphragm, where it's normally couched. But then I brought my finger over a very sharp object that was swirling around with every beat of her heart. It was protruding into the heart and into the diaphragm. I found out for sure that it was a sharp piece of wire when I cut the end of my finger.

I proceeded to *gently* retrieve the wire embedded in the apex of the left ventricle of the heart. It turned out to be a ten-inch piece of baling wire or electric fence wire. I also had to take out an eight-inch fibrinous patch that the body had produced to try to wall off the foreign object. I sewed her back up and that ended the surgery.

Young animals less than a year old are given a magnet via a pill gun to attract and hold ferrous objects, to keep the metal from getting past the reticulum. It wouldn't have helped this cow because the wire was aluminum.

I injected the cow with long-acting antibiotics and asked Dr. Whitten if he would tend to her for a few days, medically. Because of her high temperature and the possibility of postoperative infections, we agreed that she should get penicillin and streptomycin injections twice a day for five days and a daily dose of oral sulfonamides, specifically sulfanilamide.

The results were fantastic. She made a complete recovery and her heart improved immensely. When I went up there to check other cows, I would always take a listen to her heart and look her over. She never regained a completely normal heartbeat, but she was much improved after the removal of that ten-inch piece of wire.

Dr. Whitten posted that piece of wire on the bulletin board of the Department of Veterinary Sciences to remind students that hardware disease was always around. It is estimated that a hundred cows, between winter housing and summer grazing, will consume at least fifty pounds of metallic objects—nails, wires, spikes, screws—and non-metallic objects. In the early 1950s *Life* magazine had a two-page spread about a cow in England that had gone to a slaughterhouse. When the reticulum was laid open, there was everything in there from files to an alarm clock.

As Mother always said: Don't gulp your food.

22

A Boxing Lesson

One of the most colorful characters that I ever knew was a farmer named Bryce. He was a navy veteran, and like so many in that time had bought his farm through government loans after World War II.

I always remember the way Bryce dressed. He used a piece of baling twine for a belt; sometimes it was doubled up and sometimes he used two pieces. His coat came off a nearby dump; it was sleeveless and very holey. His shoes also came from the dump, and the soles were usually attached with duct tape. His trousers were also dump material, so holey the pope could have worn them. They were invariably too long or too short. Bryce would keep them rolled up to his knees in either case, through all four seasons. His fly was always open.

I never went there but the conversation always ended up with him talking about boxing. He professed to be the middleweight champion of the Seventh Fleet during the war. He said he had fought Sugar Ray Robinson, who was one of the greatest middleweights to put on boxing gloves.

Bryce would invariably start to describe one of his fights, shadow boxing and punching at the air and dancing around as he talked. One night, after we got through with some vet work and some "while-you're-here, Docs," we were standing behind my car and in he started. But with his first shadow punch he hit me right square on the mouth. It knocked me cold.

When I came to he was wiping the blood from my mouth and my nose with a wet cloth full of ice cubes and apologizing profusely. But shortly after I got to my feet he said, "Just one more thing, Doc. I want to put a ring in that bull. He's getting too big for his britches. He thinks he owns this place. He put me up against the side of the barn the other night when I was getting the cows in to milk. I had to kick him in the nose three times so I could free myself."

I asked him where the bull was and he told me it was in the night pasture. He got his old Jeep and I got my lariat, lasso, trocar, nose lead, and a bull ring. He got a pail of grain and off we went.

We criss-crossed the field a number of times and finally he spotted the bull, who was keeping company with heifers that Bryce wanted to get bred for the coming fall. Bryce took the Jeep and separated the bull from the heifers. Then he threw the grain down and the bull came to get it, eating vigorously. When he brought his head up for a moment, I caught him with the lasso around his neck and quickly tied the rope around the Jeep's bumper. He jumped around like a fish out of water, diving one way then six directions at once. I took up the slack whenever I got a break from his dancing. I finally got him fast within a couple of feet of the little Jeep. Soon I had him snug, although the Jeep kept getting pulled forward (it was in gear, with the emergency brake on). I put my right arm around his neck, took my left hand around his nose, and put the nose leader into his nostrils. He managed to put his horn into my right side (I felt that for the next six months). I immediately took the trocar, inserted it through the nasal septal cartilage, then installed the ring.

Bryce took the piece of baling twine from his belt loops and tied it on the ring. He led the thousand-pound critter back towards the barn, and by the time they got back to the barn, the bull was learning to respect the ring. Bryce led him into the barn to his stall and tied him up.

He said, "Boy he's some different animal now, Doc. That's done wonders for him. He's gonna gain some respect for this place and me from now on. You can go to the bank on that."

I said my good-byes and was on my way. A couple of weeks later I was called back to Bryce's farm for some vet work. It was a Saturday. Bryce came out of the house dressed in a Harris tweed sport coat, beautiful gray flannel slacks, and what I recall as a pair of Florsheim shoes. He looked like he just stepped out of the window of Macy's men's division. Behind Bryce came his brothe, Harold with a Polaroid camera.

Harold said, "I may as well get practiced up for the wedding." This was news! Then he said, "You and Bryce stand there side by side and let me take a picture of ya." He did. He gave me the picture. I kept it for quite a few years. The only problem was that I didn't have a picture of Bryce in his barnyard attire. The contrast would have been unbelievable.

23

A Severed Tendon and a Bootlace

I got a call one Sunday from a physician who had bought his daughter Sarah a pinto pony for her birthday. He said the pinto had cut a hock tendon clear off and could no longer put her right rear foot on the ground.

"The leg is just dangling pathetically. Can you come take a look at her?" the doctor asked.

"Yes, Doctor, it will be about three hours."

I arrived and we went to a little outbuilding. In the middle of the floor of the structure stood Nellie, a pinto pony on three legs. The right rear leg was dangling uselessly.

"She's cut completely through the deep distal flexor tendon, I believe. Am I correct?" the doctor asked.

I said, "You're exactly right, Doctor. I believe it's called the Achilles tendon in humans. It's a pretty serious injury."

I gave the little mare a shot of painkiller. Then I examined the severed ends of the tendon to find any way to reattach it. What to do? I searched my mind and discussed several surgical approaches with the physician, who was an ophthalmologist. I considered everything from stealing strips of the aponeurosis of the rectus abdominis muscle to taking some of the portion of the superficial digital flexor tendon. But in the end I considered that it would weaken these bodily structures.

I asked the doctor to go into Rockland to see if he could get some rawhide bootlaces, preferably horsehide, not cowhide.

He returned about an hour later with a pair of horsehide bootlaces, forty inches in length. I cut away pieces of the huge quadracep muscle so as to get at the proximal end of the tendon and tried to free up enough tendon to work with. On the hock end there was enough tendon already. Then I had to oppose the exposed faces of the tendons. I used #1 catgut to keep them in position and touching permanently. Using an umbilical tape needle I attached the free end of each tendon and then went about using the horsehide bootlaces that the doctor bought in Rockland to secure each end of the tendon. I took a couple of turns on the free portion of each end of the tendon. Then I took the two ends of the rawhide lace and made a tight square knot, leaving the two tendon ends attached.

I pulled as hard as I possibly could on the square knot. The two ends were still neatly touching and opposed, held in place by the catgut sutures. The doctor helped me cast the entire hock area using plaster of Paris casting material. Now the question remained whether she would bust up the whole deal when she placed her foot on the ground and put her weight on it.

However, she stepped off with her full walking gait and went for about thirty yards and came to a standing position. The doctor went into his house and returned with a flexible cloth measuring tape. We measured from the ankle, which would be a horse's tarsus, to the tip of the hoof on each leg. Eureka! They were within a tenth of an inch of each other.

I left some wound-healing oil, gave the doctor and his family instructions for limited exercise, and told them I would check on the tendon from time to time when I was in the area. The largest threat medically was the rejection of the rawhide by the horse's immune system. As in human medicine, when an organ or another body part is transplanted from one person to another individual, the donor and recipient should be matched as closely as possible. Rejection is the result of incompatibility of the recipient's proteins with the donor's. In human medicine it is common procedure to administer medications such as cyclosporine, which was developed, as are most medications, first by trial- and-error testing on animals. Such medicines to prevent rejection are usually taken on a daily basis for the lifetime of the recipient. The medicine is extremely expensive over time.

I had insisted on horsehide laces rather than cowhide in order to reduce the chance of rejection, but I was still worried that the pony would reject the bootlace, requiring a surgical removal and ruining her chance of walking normally again.

From time to time I would stop in and check her progress. We had left little windows in the cast so we could observe the healing process and watch for early signs of infection or rejection. Every time I stopped in to look at her I was more pleased. The little girl had been cantering and galloping her, really testing that connection. But it held well.

About a year later I removed the horsehide laces from the hock. Nellie the pinto came out of it fine and went on to gallop and canter at her master's will for a long time. The laces had done their work. The doctor said he made a big investment in those laces and it paid off handsomely. They had cost sixty-nine cents.

24

No Ticket!

One Saturday afternoon the phone rang. A horse had been hit in Seal Cove, Maine, by a pickup truck. Seal Cove is about seventy-five miles from Belfast. The owners of the horse tried to get veterinarians in the area to help, but none would come. So I agreed I would give it a go.

They said to come as quickly as possible—the horse was in bad shape. I jumped into my car after packing up a few things that I thought I might need and replenishing my drug supply, then I headed off for Seal Cove. At times, on the straightaways between Belfast and Bucksport, I hit eighty to eighty-five miles per hour. I was making great time. I turned right off the bridge in Bucksport, heading towards Ellsworth. I knew, from traveling those roads many, many times, that up ahead there was a hill that gradually descended and went on to a flat straightaway for about four miles. I was about halfway across it when I noticed that my speedometer was reading a hundred. And I no sooner noticed that than I saw a blue light come out from a wooded area on the side of the road.

The state trooper slowly but surely caught up with me, and when I got to the top of the hill before Ellsworth, I stopped. He asked for the usual, license and registration. By that time he had radioed ahead to the Ellsworth police, and with their red lights flashing, two Ellsworth police cruisers joined us.

One of the officers came over and started to interrogate me. I explained the situation and instead of a ticket, which I expected, the state trooper said he would escort me to Mount Desert Island, to the fork in the road that would take me to Seal Cove.

The trooper told me to follow him and hurried to his car. Following him was a panic. I could hardly keep up with him. He was hitting eighty-five or ninety most of the time. We finally came to the fork in the road after screaming across the Mount Desert Island causeway and he stopped, did a U-turn, flashed his lights three times at me, and I took off for Seal Cove while he went back towards Ellsworth.

I drove as fast as I could the rest of the way and finally came upon about thirty people gathered around a horse in the middle of the road. I knew this had to be my patient.

The horse had suffered a tremendous loss of blood due to numerous lacerations, and I noticed that its tongue was nearly cut in half. The first thing I did was ask somebody in the crowd if there was another horse around. The girl who had been riding with her friend whose horse had been hit got her own horse and brought it over. I got out my large-animal transfusion kit and took about two quarts of blood from her animal and got it into the injured horse. (In a pinch, horse-to-horse or cow-to-cow transfusions are usually safe without a blood test match. Horse-to-cow or vice-versa transfusions should not be attempted.)

I infiltrated all the major lacerations with procaine for anesthesia and proceeded to put two to three hundred stitches in that horse's body, more in the tongue than anywhere else. It took very fine suturing to work on the tongue.

But as I was suturing a laceration on the right hip I noticed that the hip was completely dislocated, so when I finished suturing I gave the horse a spinal anesthetic. With the help of a well-muscled bystander, I relocated the hip. I gave the horse some intramuscular painkiller and injected her with antibiotics, a penicillin/streptomycin combination. I taught the owner how to use the syringe and the needle, which I left with her along with the necessary medications. I also told her that if the horse didn't or couldn't get up on her own by the next morning, she might want to contact a towing service and ask them to help get the horse back on its feet using their equipment. That turned out not to be necessary as, with the help of a few neighbors, the horse got up at four A.M. the next day.

I cleaned up and had put all my gear in the trunk when a young fella came up and said, "While you're here, Doc, I have to show my horses at the Blue Hill Fair, but they have to have a test first, that anemia test." What he was referring to was an equine infectious anemia test that was required whenever horses congregated outside of their home farms. Not only did I test his horses, but once the word got out, I ended up traveling about fifteen miles around the area, testing a dozen more horses.

I finally headed for Belfast at normal posted speed limits. I arrived home at about five in the morning.

To my amazement that horse made a complete recovery over a period of six months and never showed any limp from the dislocated hip. This was another example of what a powerful healer nature is—not to mention a vet willing to risk a speeding ticket.

25

A Calving Call Starts a Busy Day

The day started at five-thirty in the morning when a farmer, Mr. Beech, called. He had a first-calf heifer who had been in labor for about two or three days and couldn't seem to have the calf. Every vet in a thirty-mile radius had been called, and they hadn't been able to save it. When I got there I saw that the tail was sticking out of the vagina and the calf was dead. That immediately told me that it was a breech, coming backwards, positioned in the mother just the way she's standing. The mother was so small in the pelvis that it was difficult to get the calf through after I'd corrected its placement. In fact, at one point I considered doing a cesarean section, but the mother's condition was rapidly deteriorating. So I worked as fast as I could to deliver the dead calf, which was a big bull calf weighing between 110 and 120 pounds. Then I turned my attention to the mother.

I was interrupted by Mrs. Beech, who said my office had called. I quickly finished and called my wife back, who told me that the Troll farm had a horse that was all cut to pieces by barbed wire and they wanted me to get there as quickly as possible. Duke was Dick Troll's favorite pulling horse. I hung the phone up and started for the door.

But first Mrs. Beech said, "Just one more thing, Doc. Could you take a look at Rex? He's itching himself to death. Has been for months. I don't know what's wrong with him. Harry's threatened to shoot him to put him out of his misery."

One look told me it was sarcoptic mange. I explained briefly what had to be done and that the next time they were in the office I'd have some medicine for him. Sarcoptic mange is hard to cure but easy to treat. A week or two later they stopped in for the medications. After a couple of months the dog's coat looked like new.

I got in my car, revved up the engine, and headed to the Troll horse farm. When I got there I couldn't believe my eyes. Duke was lying on his back, tangled up in a barbed wire fence. From his belly down it looked as if someone had gone at him with a chainsaw. When they're turned out for exercise, horses will often lie down and roll from one side to the other. This is thought to be some kind of cleansing process. But Duke had rolled too near the fence that morning, got his hind legs entangled, and then proceeded to rip his groin and the inner thighs on his big upper rear leg muscles. It was just a horrible mess, one that I remember vividly to this day.

I gave him a pre-anesthetic agent that stopped his thrashing and calmed him down a little. Dick was already at work cutting the three strands of barbed wire. After giving Duke anesthesia, we pulled the fencing out of the deep muscle wounds, and I tied off the bad bleeders (those arteries that were life- threatening) with sutures and sewed him up. About an hour and 600 stitches later he started to look like a horse again. It would be a long healing process, of course, because the muscles had been torn so deeply.

We got Duke on his feet and I gave him a shot of long-acting penicillin. I left the bottle with Dick and taught him how to inject the horse. I also gave Duke a tetanus antitoxin against lockjaw. I told Dick to stop by the office for a gallon of healing oil and explained how to use it, and reassured him that when I was out that way I would stop in to check on Duke.

Nature is a wonderful force. Within three months Duke had healed completely—even well enough so that Dick started him with light pulling and had him back in championship form for the next season. He went on to win many pulling contests with his mate.

When I arrived back at the office at about ten that morning, there were already six or eight cars in the lot for office appointments. By eleven-thirty I had taken care of eight appointments, and we had scheduled six small- animal surgeries for that day. This included a leg amputation on a dog that had been hit several days before by a ten-wheeler gravel truck, which had completely destroyed his right hind leg. I had tried for several days to save the leg but it was turning gangrenous. So that was the last surgery in the hospital.

We also had a horse coming in for a castration. Not a typical one. This horse was what is called a cryptorchid—it had a retained testicle. If left in the peritoneal cavity, the testicle would turn into a Sertoli cell tumor, which secretes the female hormon, estrogen. It can be potentially malignant.

I did the easiest surgeries first and saved the leg amputation for last. I was just completing that when I noticed a trailer drive in and knew that it must be the stallion. He would be worked on in the outdoor corral, where a lot of the large-animal surgeries were done. The testicle that doesn't descend is not usually very big, maybe as big as a middle finger. It's like hunting for a needle in a haystack in the peritoneal cavity. But I lucked out and succeeded quite quickly, took out the good testicle surgically, and within half an hour my right-hand man, the hospital manager, had the horse up on his feet. He was able to get him into the trailer after a few minutes, and they were on their way back to Lagrange, some seventy miles away.

Then I went back into the hospital and took an x-ray of a four-pound toy poodle. My forefinger and thumb had felt a gravelly texture in the bladder area, and the x-ray confirmed my suspicions that the little guy's bladder was full of stones. Half an hour later I had removed 155 stones from that little dog, none larger than a BB. One of the staff counted them as I dropped them into a bottle. Over the years I've removed many stones from many different species. The secret to preventing them is to change the alkalinity of the bladder. Stones usually form in an alkaline medium, so you have to acidify.

I always got phone calls during surgery, so I used a foot-controlled telephone-answering device, which enabled me to take calls while continuing with surgeries and treatments. I could also use this setup to talk with farmers and others who dropped in for advice. I found that if they came right into the surgery, some of them would become a little faint. I particularly remember one strapping fellow standing at six foot eight and weighing about 270 pounds. He had come in to pick up some medication and asked to speak to the doctor. My mother, the office manager, sent him out to the surgery. I was doing a rather bloody operation, as I recall, and I noticed when he started to get a little white. The next thing I knew he had fainted dead away. We elevated his feet, put a cold towel on his forehead, and he started to come around. Pretty soon he got to his feet and said, "I don't know how you stand this Doc. I'm getting out of here. See ya later."

I've had different problems with other bystanders. I was out at a farm doing a cesarean section one day, and it was quite an interesting barnyard surgery. When it came time to lift the calf out of the side of the cow's uterus, I asked the bystanders or onlookers for help. One hired man dropped his Zippo into the uterus. Another was chewing tobacco and he rolled up so much in his mouth that he couldn't spit it out. A lot of it was falling into the surgical site. Still another simply fainted away during the process. This particular cesarean section produced one of the largest calves I have ever seen. It weighed 211 pounds. This was the result of a condition known as fetal giantism. This calf was three weeks overdue and just continued to grow inside its mother. What a giant! When the case was presented to me there were two huge hooves sticking out of the vagina and that was all I could see of the 211-pound monster. All the would-be veterinarians in a thirty-mile radius had taken a crack at delivering that calf. Even the best of them couldn't budge it. They tried everything from pulling it with ropes and pulleys to using other apparatus and nothing was working. The cow needed a Cesarean.

Most of my calving cases involved cows delivering for the first time. I always jokingly suggested to farmers that they breed their first-calf heifers to nothing larger than a buck rabbit, but then I would advise them to use a Hereford or Jersey, preferably a Jersey. These produce much smaller calves on average. Unlike breeding a Holstein to a Holstein, using a Jersey bull for the first pregnancy will improve the chances of the birth being normal and should ensure that the breeding life of the heifer will be long and the deliveries uneventful.

Unfortunately, most of the time my advice wasn't taken. Holsteins produce more milk and farmers don't want a Jersey in the mix. A farmer's main concern was how much milk he could put in a bulk tank, hopefully enough to feed his family and still operate a dairy farm. So I got a lot of calls for problem deliveries.

Over the years farmers changed from using stanchion barns to providing loose housing in pole barns—open on all four sides. Sometimes the winter calving cases I worked were in temperatures as low as thirty below, with just enough wind blowing through to make it really uncomfortable. The only warmth would come from the fetal fluids and the patient herself. It felt like I would never warm up again, even running my car heater at full blast while I drove between calls.

A Calving Call Starts a Busy Day

26

TB Tests and a Head Gasket

When I got out of vet school in the mid-1950s tuberculosis was still in existence in Maine and the rest of the United States, and the Department of Agriculture started a campaign to see if the disease could be eradicated. They also wanted to eradicate brucellosis. It all involved testing cattle.

I contracted with the state's Department of Agriculture to do testing in all the towns in Waldo County, plus half the bovines in adjacent Lincoln County. The TB test involved injecting the tuberculin test agent into the caudal fold of the tail with an eighth-inch (.22 gauge) tuberculin syringe. After three days I had to go back and check every animal where it had been injected to see if it showed signs of a reaction.

A sign of infection was a severe swelling around the injection site, but it wasn't definitive because there could be other reasons for the reaction. Any suspect animal would be subjected to a more efficient diagnostic test on the neck. If that proved positive, the animal was disposed of as a nuisance to public health. The farmer was paid an indemnity for his financial loss but rarely was the full value recovered.

Tuberculosis is a disease of both man and animal. It's caused by a bacterium called *Mycobacterium tuberculosis* in humans, *m. bovis* in cattle, *m. avium* in birds. It is also known as the tubercle bacillus. It is an acid-fast bacterium and likes to live in the lungs, but it isn't restricted to that organ. It also can be found in the abdominal cavity, invading organs like the kidney and spreading throughout the entire viscera. The disease is very debilitating and the victim seems to waste away.

It was my plan to do one town a day once I got going. But I decided to get a jump-start on it by testing all the cattle in the city of Belfast, town of Waldo, and town of Knox in one day—quite an undertaking. I already did the vet work at most of these farms, knew the local roads well, and called all the farmers in advance to let them know what day I was coming and to have them spread the word among the neighbors. I'd contracted to test *all* animals—whether a large dairy or beef herd, or one or two animals belonging to an individual. So every bovine, whether it already had one or not, had to get an ear tag with an individual confirmation number related to the testing system. It turned out that the paperwork took the most time.

On a Thursday I took a helper and we started on Route 137 with a couple of big farms on that road and then turned off into Waldo and picked up a big herd there. Along the way we stopped where people had one or two cows. We came back onto Route 137 and headed for Knox, stopping as necessary. I wore catcher's leggings when I did the testing. Cattle tend to kick when you stick them with a needle, and the leggings offered some protection.

I finally arrived at Lee Larrabee's farm in Knox and tested about 250 of his cattle. I was about ready to leave when Lee said, "Just one more thing, Doc. My Belgian brood mare is due to foal today. She's overdue. Could you take a quick look at her?"

So I went to her stall, looked at her, and told Lee, "I agree with you. She's waxed heavily on her mammary glands, and I would say she is due any time."

He asked me to stop in the next morning, so at exactly seven o'clock the next morning I drove in and he greeted me, saying, "I'm glad that you're here. The mare foaled at four o'clock this morning. She had a giant colt and tore herself quite severely."

Sure enough, so I anesthetized the area and spent about forty-five minutes sewing up the tear. She looked pretty good after I got her back together.

"I'll check her in three days when I come back, Lee. If you have any questions, let me know."

He said, "Fine."

My helper and I then took off for Belfast and arrived there at about quarter to eight in the morning to start another busy day at the hospital with whatever was to happen. I hoped that Sunday would be a lighter day for me, since I needed to re-check all those cattle.

The next day it started to snow lightly. Then the snow began to fall harder—right through Saturday afternoon. When I got up at four on Sunday morning, about twenty inches of snow had fallen and the temperature had dropped down to ten degrees. The wind-chill factor made it feel like twenty degrees below zero.

I decided that I had better not use my practice's car to get around that day. I had an old four-wheel-drive Willis Overland with a manual plow on the front end, which would be a better choice for this particular Sunday.

I picked up my helper, Dave, and we set out to retrace our travels from Wednesday and Thursday. We arrived at Hill's and Bowen farm on Route 137 in Belfast without incident. The herd was in two different housings. There was a main barn and behind it a slightly smaller barn that contained almost as many cattle as the big barn. I dropped the plow down and plowed right up to the second barn, which I intended to read first. I almost got to the door of the old barn when I heard a tremendously loud bang from the engine. I had an idea what had happened, but Harry Bowen came running out of the house because he thought he'd heard a gun being fired in his yard.

Harry threw open the hood of the Jeep and said what I already knew. The head gasket was blown. That put an end to my plans for the day.

Then I remembered that Joe Johnson, a car dealer, lived just across the road from this farm. I went over to Joe's and told him about my predicament. He was very sympathetic.

"I'll tell you what I can do. I can let you use my wife's pickup. She just uses it to go to town," he offered. "I can let you have that today for thirty cents a mile."

I said, "Joe, you've got a deal. I appreciate what you're doing." He proceeded to throw in four five-gallon cans of gas for our trip. I tossed my practice grip into the truck and we were off.

Eventually we reached Knox and turned into Lee Larrabee's place to check his cattle.

He said, "I'm glad to see you. The mare's doing fine, but I'd like to have you check her while you're here, Doc."

I went into the stall and looked over the mare and the new colt. Both were doing fine. While I was doing that I told Lee what had happened with my Jeep, because he had asked about the unfamiliar pickup.

Lee said, "That's too bad, Doc. If you need anything, I'll be glad to provide it for you."

I said, "That's all right, Lee, I'm all set."

We proceeded to read the tests on the entire town of Knox. When we got back to the office and checked the records, I saw that I had accomplished what I had set out to do. I had tested and read 2,200 head of cattle and young stock on Route 137, the towns of Waldo and Knox, and the city of Belfast. And we hadn't found one suspicious animal.

Four days later, I drove into my yard in the early morning light after a busy night of farm rounds, and was astounded to see my old dilapidated Jeep sitting there. The key was in it. It started it up on the first try and was running quieter than it had in years.

Unbeknownst to me, Lee Larabee had gone to Harry Bowen's with his big GMC truck, winched the Jeep on board, and took it to his machine shop, where he replaced the blown gasket. Over the years I've seen Lee tear apart everything from 200-horsepower diesel tractors to small gasoline tractors. There was nothing he couldn't fix.

A few days later I had go to his farm to treat a cow, and it gave me a chance to say, "Lee, thank you! What was that work worth to you?"

He said, "You don't owe me anything."

I said, "You don't fool me." I had seen that "gotcha" grin coming over his face.

"You were surprised, weren't you?"

"I nearly fainted when I got out of my car and saw the Jeep in the yard. But I've checked around on how much a gasket job costs on a four-cylinder, and I'm giving you $250 against your vet bill."

He said, "That's more than fair. You're getting the worse end of the bargain."

I replied, "The hell I am. In addition to that, I want to thank you from the bottom of my heart."

He simply said, "Anytime."

I finished TB testing the two adjoining counties over the next couple of months by patching it in with other vet calls in the different towns. In all the years of my practice I found only six suspicious TB animals. Three eventually proved to be infected, all in one herd of animals kept in close proximity, and the three had to be destroyed. I would estimate, conservatively, that in all the years of my practice I tested over 20,000 head of cattle.

27

A B-52 in the Eye

A rather frantic woman called me one afternoon from Hudson, Maine, a little town near Orono and west of Old Town. I was her regular vet for the horse farm they ran, and had been for a long time.

It seems her boys were playing baseball in the pasture and one of the bigger boys hit a line drive that struck their brood mare in the eye and knocked her cold. She said the eye looked as if it were going to pop out of the socket—she thought the eye was ruined for good. Could I come right away?

I told her, "Keep ice packed on it until I get there."

"How soon can you get here?" she asked, anxiously but nicely.

"I'll be flying up, and you should meet me at the Old Town Airport in forty-five minutes. I'll be flying in my own plane."

I went to the Belfast Airport after packing my medical grip with what I anticipated needing to treat the mare. I filed a flight plan in the little airport office, then got a sectional map of the flight path to Old Town Airport. When non-fliers look into the sky, they see only a sunny day, blue sky, and sometimes clouds of various shapes and sizes. When a flier looks up, he or she sees a maze of sky roads, or skyways, and knows that he or she must adhere to the rules of these sky roads. There is little room for error up there.

I opted to fly VFR (visual flight rules) because it was such a clear day. If necessary I could resort to instrument flight rules, since my plane had the proper instruments. I quickly drew my vector lines on the sectional map to fly east to the mouth of the Penobscot River, turn left and follow the river to Brewer, then follow the last vector to Old Town Airport. There was just one catch. Dow Air Force Base was operational then, and it had B-52 bombers and F-101 Voodoo fighters taking off and landing all the time. Civilian planes had to get a clearance to pass anywhere close to their climbing corridor.

I radioed the Bangor tower when I was about three miles away. The controller reported there was no aircraft traffic expected for at least a half-hour and cleared me through the climbing corridor.

I hadn't more than signed off the radio when my cockpit suddenly became dark. Directly in front of me was a B-52, an awesome sight from a distance, but truly frightening up close and in the air near you. It seemed to get closer and louder every second. I felt my plane shudder from the vortex of its eight engines. The plane was so low and close at one point that I could see the rivets and read all the little signs like "No Step," "Do Not Walk Here," "Jet Fuel Only," "Crew Entrance Only," and "Stand Clear."

I was barely able to keep my little plane in the air. It started spinning out of control from the turbulence created by the giant B-52. The spin was getting worse. My pilot training took over instantly and I recalled my flight instructor's warning: "Spins end up fatal if not corrected ASAP."

The plane was spinning clockwise, so I gave her hard left rudder and full right aileron. We continued spinning toward Mother Earth. In desperation I pushed the wheel hard and nose-dived. When I was about 300 to 400 feet from crashing into an electric substation, the plane finally came out of its spin. I said out loud, "Thank you, God," and continued on to Old Town Airport.

Some minutes later I met the owner of the mare at the airport and we sped off toward the patient. She had described the mare's situation very well. The eye and the orbital socket which holds the eye were completely banged up. The ball had hit the horse dead center in the eyeball and had nearly exploded it. The eye was swelling and starting to protrude out of the orbit. It was an ugly-looking mess.

The first thing I did was anesthetize the eye and then set about to suture a few pieces of the sclera together. I actually had to suture back one lateral muscle of the eyeball, which had ruptured. I then injected dexamethasone, a steroid, into the swollen edematous area where all the soft tissue was severely injured. After that injection I gave some systemic dexamethasone, along with a heavy dose of three-day antibiotic. Then came a small dose of amphetamine, a stimulant to help get the mare back up on her feet. Within twenty minutes the mare was standing by herself. Slowly but surely we got her back into the stable and she seemed to be aware of her surroundings.

When I thought it was safe to leave the mare, I packed up my things and we got into the client's vehicle for the trip back to the airport. Five minutes later I was airborne and headed back to Belfast.

Three days later I made an uneventful return flight to Old Town, and again a week later. The eye had improved fifty percent by this juncture. I left them a big bottle of eyedrops that contained an antibiotic and dexamethasone solution. I asked the client to call me in a week's time and let me know how things were going. When she did call she said it was like a miracle. The mare had recovered her vision and was returning to normal pasture life.

If I had collided with that B-52, it would have been disastrous for me but probably wouldn't have brought down the bomber. That close call still flashes in front of me occasionally, and my stomach gets a funny feeling.

A B-52 in the Eye

28

A Miracle Cow

One early June morning at four A.M., the bedside phone awakened me from a deep sleep. "Vet'nary Brown?" said a husky female voice.

I mumbled that it was indeed I.

"This is Libby Johnson. We just found a cow down with milk fever and she's cast her withers. Linton's been looking for her for three days and just found her this morning, barely alive. Can you come right out?"

A half-hour later I pulled into the Johnson's dooryard in the town of Waldo. Sunrise was tinting the clouds a deep pink and the air held the scent of new leaves. Spring comes late to the hill towns of coastal Maine, but when it finally arrives, it's worth the wait.

Linton Johnson strode to my car as I was opening the trunk to get out my field kit and pail. His face reflected none of the joy of spring. "She's down into the swamp in the back pasture," he reported, his mouth set in a grim line.

Like other animals, cows will, given the chance, seek out the most isolated place to give birth, which is why Linton hadn't been able to find his cow for several days. We tied a ten-gallon milk can full of warm water on the drawbar of the tractor and headed for the swamp. Twenty minutes later we'd gone as far as we could drive and proceeded on foot, each gripping one side handle of the milk can and sharing my gear. The weight sank us knee-deep in black swamp ooze with every third step, and black flies, the small biting insects that plague Maine's woods in May and June, began to swarm around our heads. Neither of us had a free hand to swat them and I could feel maddening welts swelling on my neck.

"Fella says a whole family disappeared trying to cross this swamp, way back," Linton said.

"No kidding," I said.

"Ayuh," he mused. "Mosquitoes and black flies ate 'em to pieces, I reckon, else'n they just sank into the mud." Sure enough, the black flies soon merged with a whining cloud of mosquitoes.

Linton, an avid hunter, knew this territory well. "Shot a deer right here last fall," he said as we slogged through thigh-high bog water.

"There she is, Doc," he cried a moment later. "That's Clara over there, on that little island of swale grass."

By now the sun was well up, and the day promised to be beastly hot and sticky. Linton and I were soaked from the neck to the waist in perspiration, and from the waist down in swamp water. On the wet but solid ground where the sick cow lay, we set down our gear and began swatting the squadrons of insects on our arms and heads. "Damn, Doc, " Linton said, "now I know how those poor boys in Vietnam must feel in them rice paddies."

Clara could have been easily mistaken for dead, and I credited Linton for detecting her faint heartbeat. Her odds were dire, and I told Linton that. We both knew that the other option was for Linton to shoot her. "I know she's hanging on by a thread," he said, "but she's a damn good milker, Doc. Give it your best shot."

So we set about trying to revive the poor cow. First I injected intravenous heart stimulants. I then asked Linton to act as an IV stand by holding up a bottle of calcium solution which flowed into the cow's jugular through a large needle linked to the bottle by a rubber tube. We then pumped a second bottle of calcium-dextrose solution into her the same way. These desperately needed nutrients lifted her spirits considerably, and she found the energy to flick her tail. The flies and mosquitoes were devouring her as well as us.

Trying not to think about the swarming insects, I stripped off my sodden shirt and lay belly-down in the swamp grass. With Linton's help and a great deal of difficulty I managed to insert the swollen and damaged uterus back into the cow. The organ had deteriorated, having been exposed to the elements and the insects for at least thirty-six hours. I didn't like the looks of it. Meanwhile, the voracious bugs had found my bare torso. I scrambled up from the muck and yanked my muddy, wet shirt back on. The cow, exhausted by my ministrations, had laid her head back down on the wet grass. Her eyes were closed against the flies.

"Think she's got a chance, Doc?" Linton asked.

"I'll be honest, Linton," I said. "That poor beast is one of the sickest animals I've ever seen alive. I've done what I can, and let's just say she's in the Maker's hands now."

"But you gave her the right medicines, didn't you?"

"Yes, but it may be too late to prevent irreversible metabolic stasis."

"What's that?"

"Well, it's like when an airplane loses power in flight and goes into a nose dive. The pilot might manage to get the engine started again and pull up on the nose, but after a certain point in the descent, it's not going to do any good," I explained.

Linton sighed. "I reckon I oughta take a look around for her calf," he said. "I ain't seen hide nor hair of it."

For about fifteen minutes we searched in a wide circle, looking for signs of Clara's baby. There was no sign of the placenta (afterbirth), but it's not unusual for ruminants to eat the afterbirth to prevent predators from finding and killing their newborns. Calves are able to walk only minutes after being born, but this boggy terrain would have been tough walking for such a young calf.

Convinced that coyotes had probably gotten the calf, we finally gave up and sat down on a hummock of grass to wait for the medication to have an effect on poor Clara. After a few minutes, Linton spoke. "You believe in faith healing, Doc?"

"Well, I believe that you should always apply medical treatment first," I replied. "That's how I was trained."

I got up and walked over to the stricken cow lying on her side in the swamp grass. I stared down at her, hoping for a sign of change. But she didn't so much as move an eyelash. Only the slow rise and fall of her ribcage let me know she was still alive.

"I don't think it hurts to pray," Linton allowed.

I nodded. "I'm not much of a praying man, but I have seen a few miracles," I said. Linton looked at me expectantly. "I once examined a dog that had been run over by an eighteen-wheeler. The owner saw it happen. The dog got right up out of the road and ran back into the driveway, and the owner brought him right to me. He didn't have any internal injuries or broken bones, only a cut on his forehead. As far as I know, he's alive today."

I squatted down next to Clara and placed my hand on her forehead. "This is one of those times I wish I was one of those faith healers," I said. "Then I could just put a hand on her head and say, 'Rise, rise, rise!'"

No sooner did the last "rise" come out of my mouth than Clara picked up her head, churned her feet in the muck, and sat up on her brisket. With a mighty thrust she rolled to her feet and, in the same motion, took off across the swamp in calcium-dextrose overdrive.

For the next hour we chased the cow all over that swamp, and probably we'd still be pursuing her if she hadn't finally come to the edge of the stream that fed the swamp and stopped abruptly. Linton quickly removed his belt as I grabbed Clara by her horns. Between the two of us, we fastened the long belt around her neck, just as she leapt into the stream—taking us with her. Linton gripped the belt where it met her neck, and I had a hold on the lower portion when we plunged in, the water rising over our waists.

"Better keep her headed upstream, Doc," Linton gasped, as we each tried to keep one hand on the belt. "There's higher ground just ahead."

Too many times our feet never touched bottom, and I'm sure Clara shared our near panic. Though I doubt she meant to, there were a few times when it seemed like she was trying to drown all three of us. She finally made for shore and we ended up on solid ground. Still holding firmly to the belt, we guided her through the woods and about three-quarters of an hour later reached the barn—drenched, exhausted, and covered with insect bites.

After we led Clara to her stall, Linton's wife, Juanita, greeted us in the yard. "Well, don't you fellas look like a pair of drowned rats," she said, laughing. Linton, who had so far maintained a pretty good sense of humor, shot her a glaring look. Juanita ignored him. "Linton, did you find Clara's calf?"

Linton shook his head. "Reckon the coyotes got him."

I went into the milkroom and started washing up. Just then Juanita burst into the milkroom, followed by Linton. "Seth just called," she cried breathlessly. "He says there's a calf running crazy all over the pasture with his cows." Seth Green was the next-door neighbor.

"He noticed one of his best cows wasn't giving as much milk as she shoulda been the last few days, and sure enough, that little one of Clara's was sucking on her," Juanita told me. "Seth's gonna bring him over, by and by."

I smiled. "Another miracle."

Juanita looked blank until Linton explained what had happened with Clara in the swamp. She snorted out a laugh.

"Better go down to get the tractor," he told her. "Our stuff's still down there. You'll find it if you just follow our path. And take my wadin' boots—you're gonna need 'em."

Juanita went to the corner where the rubber boots stood and tugged them on without a word. She neither smiled nor complained. It was just another day in the life of a Maine farmer's wife.

A few minutes later, Seth pulled into the driveway with the calf in the back seat of his beat-up Ford station wagon. An older man, he eased himself out of the driver's seat, then ambled to the back door and lifted out the calf, leading the spunky little critter by a piece of baling twine over to Linton.

"There ya go, li'l fella," said Seth. Then he spotted me. "Hey, Doc," he said. "How ya doin'?"

"Pretty good, Seth," I answered. "You?"

"Shucks," he said, removing an ancient feed cap and scratching his bald head, "I'm doing pretty good, but my dog's got a growth on his head. I'm hopin' it ain't cancer. Maybe you can take a look at it, seein's how you're right here, Doc."

"Okay, sure," I said.

Seth nodded and shuffled his feet. "Then maybe you can check my draft mare. See if she's pregnant," he said.

"All right," I said. "Let's go."

I got my spare pail and some extra gear out of the back seat of my car, and got into his car. He drove at a crawl, and I feared we'd be broadsided by an oncoming car as we crossed the road. Just as we pulled into Seth's driveway, one zoomed by and honked in warning.

"Goddamn young fellas," he muttered, "always in a hurry."

"Yeah," I agreed, to be polite. "By the way, aren't you getting close to retirement age? You've been at this farming business awhile."

"As the fella says, I'm gonna retire three days after I die," he said. "Besides, I don't even know how old I am."

"Really?"

"I asked my sister Selma not too long ago. She lives down 'n the city." He paused. The city in question was probably Portland. "She allowed I was a year older 'n her."

"Oh—so you do know how old you are," I said.

Seth braked to a stop in front of his ancient, sagging barn and turned off the engine. "Nope," he said. "She didn't say how old she was."

I decided not to pursue this line of conversation. As we stepped out of the car, I noticed Seth's old black dog sunning himself in the dooryard. I bent to feel the growth on the top of his head—an abscess. "Well, Seth, it's not cancer," I told him. "We can take care of this in two shakes."

The old man smiled, revealing a toothless lower jaw. "Mighty good news, Doc."

Asking Seth to hold Blackie's head, I swabbed the abscess, which was nothing more than a pocket of pus that had formed around an infected puncture wound, probably from a cat bite or scratch. After injecting a topical anesthetic near the swelling, I asked Seth to talk soothingly to Blackie as I fished a scalpel out of my pail.

"He won't feel this, Seth," I reassured him. "But we're all going to smell it." With that I lanced the abscess, releasing a blob of putrid yellow pus.

"You ain't kiddin'," Seth remarked, crinkling his nose at the rank odor.

I swabbed out the wound with alcohol-soaked cotton, and then filled the shallow pit in Blackie's head with antibiotic ointment, handing it to Seth when I was done. "Put that on twice a day for a week or so, and make sure the wound is healing," I told him. If the infection had left a deeper hole, I would have inserted a gauze wick to keep the wound open at the top so as to ensure healing from the inside out.

We then entered the decrepit barn, where I checked his draft mare for pregnancy and found her to be with foal. These two events cheered Seth considerably, and I left him smiling and looking pleased with his domain.

I crossed the road back to the Johnson place just as Juanita was pulling up in front of the barn on the tractor, bearing my equipment. Linton strolled out of the milkroom, having succeeded in washing much of the swamp muck from his shoes and overalls. "Hey, Doc," he said, "with all that commotion I kinda forgot. I was wonderin' if while you're here you could castrate White Tail."

Linton had told me about his pet deer once before, shortly after he'd discovered the day-old fawn in his field, orphaned after poachers had shot the mother out of season. Linton had a reputation for shooting his share of deer year-round, and I wondered about White Tail's new home and the Johnsons' taste for venison. But the fawn had apparently grown into a two-year-old, 150-pound buck, and in the process Linton had become fond of him.

"He's gettin' kinda frisky with them antlers, now that he's of age," Linton said, pulling up his wet pant legs to reveal long vertical scabs on his shins. White Tail had obviously been sharpening his antlers in the male deer's rutting, or mating, ritual.

"Seems like he's mistaken you for a tree trunk," I said.

"I don't mind that so much, Doc," Linton said. "I just didn't want him to head back to the woods this fall and go girlin' on me. I can't stand the thought of some hunter shootin' my Little Willie."

"Little Willie?"

"Oh, that's what I call him for short," Linton explained.

"Well, if you can hold him long enough for me to get a shot into him, I'll give it a try," I said.

Linton collected some apples, Willie's favorite dessert, from the kitchen and went to the edge of the field. He whistled and held up an apple. The buck materialized in a matter of minutes, and Linton coaxed him into the milkroom, which contained a large stainless-steel sink and a milk cooler—a low covered tank, also of stainless-steel, about the size of four bathtubs. The room's only openings were a door and a narrow window about five feet off the floor. While we humans thought it was a good idea to huddle together in the fifteen-by-fifteen-foot space, White Tail didn't.

As I readied my anesthetic syringe, he scraped his hooves on the floor and flung his body this way and that. Spying the window, he jumped wildly towards it, feet flying like Rudolph the Red-nosed Reindeer. The glass seemed to explode as White Tail crashed through it, and we flinched against a shower of shattered window-panes. When we looked up a second later, there was White Tail's rear end stuck in the opening, his feet thrashing. He had almost escaped, but his hips didn't quite fit.

Linton and I grabbed his flailing hind legs and I tried to inject anesthesia into his muscle. But White Tail must have had eyes in his feet, because he swatted that syringe across the room, where it smashed on the cement floor. These were the days of glass syringes.

We wrestled him into the milkroom, trying not to cut him on the jagged glass. By now adrenaline was pumping through the buck's veins. He crashed wildly about the room in panic, bouncing off the walls, into the big steel sink, into the ceiling. In close quarters he was no longer the tame Little Willie, but the wild animal Linton had found in the field. His only thought was to escape, apparently at any price. Blood flowed from several cuts and scrapes, and his collisions with the cement-block walls were no doubt leaving nasty bruises.

A Miracle Cow

Linton and I dove behind the milk cooler for a quick conference. "He's startin' to really hurt himself, Doc," Linton said.

"Yeah," I agreed. "We're just going to have to wrangle him like a young bull."

"Okay, count of three, I'll take the horns, you take the legs," he said.

At three we stood up and lunged for Little Willie. Linton scored, getting a strong grip on the antlers. I wasn't so lucky. My hand gripped one leg, but my forehead stopped his other foot. With that my own adrenaline kicked in, and I managed to get hold of the free foot. Linton tipped the buck's head to the side, and Willie WhiteTail had no choice but to lower himself to the floor. I fished another syringe out of my pail and somehow managed to load it again, injecting it into his hind end.

Normally the castration would have taken only fifteen minutes, but Willie White Tail turned out to have only one testicle, which meant the other one was lodged somewhere in his abdomen. This in turn meant surgery. Linton urged me to go ahead, so I proceeded. A half-hour later, I had removed them both and was dabbing brine on his cuts—none of them serious. And the buck started to stir. A few minutes later he staggered to his feet and Linton led him to his private paddock behind the barn. I'd like to say that Willie White Tail lived a long and happy life, but night hunters poached him off Linton's front lawn three years later.

Clara however, survived without problems and continued to be one of Linton's best milkers for years. He took pride in saying that she must have been tougher than a boiled owl.

Driving home that day, I reflected over what I'd done and was thankful for the outcome. I must confess that not all cases went my way. On balance I won my share, but I always wondered what I did right and why something would go wrong, and looked for ways to improve myself throughout it all. I had to win enough to keep a clear conscience and keep myself going with my busy schedule.

When I did win a big one it would bring me back to my youth, to my days on the family farm. My grandfather would send me to the field with the draft horses. After plowing the field he would always inspect it. I remember once, after a long, hot day of plowing for both the horses and me, he went out, looked the field over and then came to see me in the stable where I was taking the harnesses off the horses.

"Son, that was a good job of plowing," he said to me. "I couldn't have plowed a straighter furrow myself." And that kind of praise from my grandfather was very rare. It put me on cloud nine and gave me a great deal of confidence.

When I was at vet school I had the greatest teacher in the world for learning diagnostic medicine, Francis Fox at Cornell. He was a professor of large-animal medicine, taught diagnostic procedures, and was brilliant in every aspect. He gave me a lot of extra help during my four years there and inspired me to try to do my best all the time. He became a conscience whispering in my ear, and my animal patients were always better for his voice.

When a large-animal veterinarian drives into a farmer's yard to treat a sick cow he has very little in the way of diagnostic tools. He has his five senses, basically, and a stethoscope—and human nature. Without it you might as well not go into practice. I never left home without it.

Acknowledgments

I greatly appreciate the kindness and support of Arlene Wheelock, who opened her home and heart to me and helped make my writing environment the best it could be.

I would also like to thank:

Ed Hoyt III, who put in countless hours transcribing my stories for this second volume. His tenacity and intelligence have been valuable contributions.

Laurah Jeanine Brown, my youngest daughter, who provided a lot of support and help throughout this project. I thank her immensely.

My four grandchildren, Sarah, Jessica, Julius, and Dakota, for providing me with the inspiration to put these stories in writing. I am blessed that Julius and Dakota have lived with me over the years. A lot of people say, "Grandchildren. Wow, they come, they visit, they leave." But Julius and Dakota have stayed around, and it's been my greatest joy. All of my grandchildren are marvelous children who are serious about education, which pleases me no end.

Jean Roy Gay, who put countless hours into my practice. She was always on the phone keeping the appointments straight and moving the practice forward. This was not easy in a practice with both large and small animals. Her efforts have never been forgotten by me, and I greatly appreciate them to this day.

Trudy Chambers Price, whose sharp mind and literary skills are amongst the best. I thank her for reading my manuscript! She is the author of the book, *The Cows Are Out! Two Decades on a Maine Dairy Farm*. It is a great book and I highly recommend it.

I would also like to dedicate *Just One More Thing, Doc* to the Cornell College of Veterinary Medicine Class of 1956, with whom I was fortunate enough to graduate. Many of them went into large-animal practice and might well have written this book themselves. We've all had the same experiences, and the only difference is that I've had the time to write down a few of my stories. I'm sure each one of them has his own stories to tell.

BRADFORD B. BROWN, DVM, grew up on a farm in Vassalboro, Maine, and like two of his brothers, graduated from the Cornell University College of Veterinary Medicine. He joined his brother Phil's veterinary practice in Belfast, Maine, where they worked together for thirteen years, and then continued on his own for ten more, running a small-animal hospital and making hundreds of farm calls. Retired now and living at the family farm in Vassalboro, he's been remembering the people and animals and the many adventures he enjoyed.